# Building the Body

*Learning Activities for Growing Congregations*

Steve Aisthorpe, Lesley Hamilton-Messer, David McCarthy,
Phill Mellstrom, Robbie Morrison and Rob Rawson

*Published on behalf of*
THE CHURCH OF SCOTLAND
MISSION AND DISCIPLESHIP COUNCIL

SAINT ANDREW PRESS
Edinburgh

First published in 2019 by Saint Andrew Press
SAINT ANDREW PRESS
121 George Street
Edinburgh EH2 4YN

ISBN 978 0 7152 0974 5

British Library Cataloguing in Publication Data
A catalogue record for this book is available from the
British Library.

It is the publisher's policy to use only papers that are natural and
recyclable and that have been manufactured from timber grown in
renewable, properly managed forests. All of the manufacturing
processes of the papers are expected to conform to the
environmental regulations of the country of origin.

Typeset by Regent Typesetting Ltd
Printed and bound in the United Kingdom by
CPI Group (UK) Ltd

# Contents

# Acknowledgements

*Building the Body* was written and compiled by staff of the Church of Scotland Mission and Discipleship Council: Steve Aisthorpe, Lesley Hamilton-Messer, David McCarthy, Phill Mellstrom, Robbie Morrison and Rob Rawson.

Special thanks are owed to Philip Hillyer for his work in preparing the manuscript, and for keeping a diverse team of contributors focused on the task at hand.

Sincere thanks also go to Diane Knowles for her patient and diligent assistance. Finally, but by no means least, thanks to the many mentors, teachers and writers whose collective wisdom has informed all that we have done here.

# You are not alone

All who have collaborated in creating this book are genuinely excited by the potential of these activities being more widely available. If you are a facilitator using these activities and would like to be in touch with others, you are warmly invited to join the Building the Body Facebook Group at: www.facebook.com/Building-the-Body-735800873453062. You can post any questions there, share your experiences and tips, find or share additional ideas or resources. Welcome to the community of facilitators.

# Read This First!

If you have already read some sections of this book before you have arrived at this page, that's OK. People interact with books in a whole variety of ways. With a book like this, it would be common to flick through, getting an overview, perhaps reading a few sections. Will it be useful? Will it be easy to use?

So why the bold instruction at the top of this page?

When the six of us who have collaborated to produce this book first talked about the idea that eventually became this book, we had a vision. Having each led workshops, trainings, retreats and conferences with a variety of churches, Christian groups and organisations over many years, we had devised, borrowed, adapted, used and collected a lot of ideas, tools, techniques and resources. We had all used things that we would never use again. We had all discovered other activities which had surprised us in their effectiveness to foster a deepening and strengthening of people's relationship with God and each other – and others that had proved to be excellent at enabling people to understand their community better and discern their part in God's mission better. Our vision was to share these activities and our experiences in facilitating them with others. With you, for example.

In this book we have drawn together activities which encourage active listening, arouse curiosity and creativity, inspire prayerful reflection, assist better understanding of others, bring together different perspectives … and much more. They have all been thoroughly road tested. In our experience, not only do they often lead to profound insights and experiences, they are also usually a lot of fun! Each person involved in this book really wishes that they had discovered a book like this when they started out working with groups, congregations and organisations. We are genuinely excited by the idea of you and others like you taking these activities and using them with groups of people. The potential is tremendous.

However, the reason we want you to read this page is not because we want to tell you how amazing this book is. Rather, we want to warn you that you are in danger of wasting your time. Worse still, you could waste the time and effort and good will of many others too. You could waste some perfectly good opportunities, because, in the words of 1980s girl band Bananarama, 'It ain't what you do, it's the way that you do it … And that's what gets results.' When we sent out the draft chapters of this book to people and asked for some feedback, time and again they told us that the activities are great, the instructions are clear, but whether they are effective or not depends on how well they are facilitated.

But panic not. You can be a great facilitator. You probably have most of the skills you need. Those you don't have you can develop. And you are not alone. As you will discover, buying this book is also your invitation to join a community of like-minded facilitators and would-be facilitators online, enabling us all to learn from one another and grow together.

Unless you are a very experienced facilitator, we strongly urge you to read and digest the section on 'Facilitation Made Easy'. If you *are* exceptionally experienced, you will want to read it anyway, as you will know that there is always more to learn and you will be constantly on the lookout for new insights and ideas.

The book is divided into six main sections: 1 Reflecting on Whose We Are, 2 Knowing One Another, 3 Exploring Our Cultures, 4 Understanding Our Communities, 5 Learning from Our Experiences, 6 Discerning Our Future. These sections reflect the scope of the book and each includes some of our favourite activities in relation to that particular purpose. However, many of the activities can be adapted for a variety of purposes. So please view this book as a tool box, a collection of activities from which you can select and mix and modify to serve your purposes.

And finally, two vital reminders. First, 'be alert and always keep on praying' (Eph. 6:18). Remember to weave practices of prayer into all you do. How that is expressed will vary according to your own habits and the traditions of the people you use these activities with. Second, seek to be motivated and enlivened and guided by God's love that 'has been poured out into our hearts through the Holy Spirit' (Rom. 5:5). For, 'if my facilitation skills are legendary, but I do not have love, I am only an annoying noise … if I have the most stimulating and thought-provoking activities imaginable, but do not have love, I am nothing … if I plan programmes that are renowned as inspiring and energising, but do not have love, I gain nothing … But love never fails.'

Happy reading and blessed facilitating.

Steve Aisthorpe, Lesley Hamilton-Messer, David McCarthy,
Phill Mellstrom, Robbie Morrison and Rob Rawson
July 2018

# Facilitation Made Easy

## Facilitation?

'Facilitation' means, quite simply, 'to make something easy'. In the context of the activities in this book it means:

- Putting people at ease.
- Encouraging an attitude of prayerful expectation and openness to what God might be showing or saying or doing in and through the activity.
- Ensuring that healthy group dynamics enable everyone to participate in ways that are comfortable for them.
- Helping people achieve their aim.
- Encouraging people to listen actively to others and to share openly with others.
- Helping people to value and express their unique perspectives and experiences.

## DIY or external?

All the activities in this book can be facilitated by a person (or persons) from within the group or congregation – or by asking someone else to come and do this. There are potential benefits and drawbacks with both approaches. Facilitators from within the group or congregation will know the people involved and may be able to use that knowledge to manage the group dynamics well. However, an insider may find it difficult to serve the needs of the group without getting involved themselves. Even if they are willing to sacrifice their own participation in order to enable others to make a full contribution, they may not be viewed as sufficiently neutral by others.

Using people from outside the group or congregation may reduce the likelihood of people feeling that the facilitator(s) might be bringing their own agenda. However, external facilitators will need to work harder to get to know the people and to understand how the group functions.

# Who can be a facilitator?

For someone to be an effective facilitator, they need to be committed to the idea of enabling others to bring their best possible contribution to an activity. In addition, they need to be able to do the following:

- Plan and prepare the programme and resources with care.
- Put people at ease and guide them through an activity while being sensitive to individual needs and the dynamics of groups.
- Communicate effectively by giving clear verbal instructions and, in some cases, in writing, e.g. recording feedback on a flip chart.

In addition, for people to facilitate effectively within their own context, they need to be well regarded and have the trust of people. Whatever role facilitators normally have within the group or congregation, they will need to ensure that all involved know that every person's opinion is of equal value. If those in formal leadership positions are to be effective facilitators they will need to emphasise this.

# Solo or team?

Even in a small group there are multiple benefits in having more than one facilitator. Firstly, it spreads the workload. Different people can take the lead for different activities. That means less preparation is required by each person. Participants will also appreciate a variety in presentation style and voice. Secondly, having more than one facilitator means that, while one person takes the lead on a particular activity, the other(s) can have their eyes and ears wide open, giving their full attention to how people are responding, observing whether they are understanding instructions and looking out for people who may be struggling to participate or people who might tend to dominate or disrupt.

Another advantage of the team approach is that, while no one person may have all the necessary skills, a pair or a small team may feel that, together, they have all the qualities that are needed. For example, one person may be happy to lead sessions, but would prefer not to create or prepare resources; someone else may be happy to take the role of observing from the edge and gently intervening to guide or support, but be unwilling to take a more up-front role in giving instructions.

# Planning for facilitation

Effective facilitators give careful attention to each of the following areas, having each of them in mind as they plan, as they prepare and as they facilitate:

**Why?** What is the **purpose** of this activity and what kind of outcomes or benefits are we looking for? Each of the exercises in this book contains a clear indication of its purpose, which should assist in selecting the most useful.

**How?** What is the **process** by which we are going to achieve this purpose or attain these outcomes or benefits? The instructions provided for each exercise give step-by-step details of the process. There is also a list of resources and equipment required.

**Who?** Who are the **people** involved, how might group dynamics aid or challenge the process, are there any special needs within the group to consider? For example, do any of the participants have limitations in terms of mobility, sight or hearing? How will you ensure that everyone is able to be safe, comfortable and able to participate fully?

## Planning the programme

Once you are clear about the why, how and who, it is time to select the activities that are going to be most helpful. Just as people are well-advised to 'warm up' before attempting serious physical exercise, so, if we want people to interact effectively, it is wise to begin by easing people into conversation and developing the sense of being part of a group. Activities from the 'Knowing One Another' section of this book are effective in helping people to enjoy being together and to build confidence and trust.

When drafting your programme, consider which activities might be demanding for the group or when there is a risk of energy levels dipping. Then think about when it might be timely to build in a break, some refreshment or an activity which the group will find energising. In the earlier part of a programme you may want to use activities that will open people's minds and generate ideas; in the later stages it may be appropriate to select activities that help to narrow down, focus in, discern or prioritise. With the purpose of the programme in mind, and aware of the people you will be facilitating, consider carefully how and when to incorporate prayer, quiet reflection and worship. Think of your programme as a menu, with starters, main course, dessert and perhaps something refreshing to help wash it down!

## Punctuality and preparation

When we start and finish at the promised times we demonstrate that we value people's time. Allow realistic time for the activities; don't try to cram in too much. The phrase 'less is more' may sound paradoxical, but when it comes to the kinds of activities in this book it is invariably true. Ensure that you have adequate time to set up the space in an appropriate way, arrange necessary resources and set up and check any equipment. How the space is arranged when people arrive shapes their expectations. If people need to be able to see a flip chart, a screen or some kind of visual aid, ensure that everyone has a clear line of sight.

Many of the activities in this book are designed for use in small groups. Unless stated otherwise, ensure that groups comprise between four and seven people. If the group is larger than this, it will take longer for all to contribute and, when discussion is involved, there can be a tendency for larger groups to operate as two groups or for some people to remain disengaged. If you plan times of plenary discussion or feedback, be aware that the time required is proportional to the size of the group. If, as the first people arrive, you are calm, welcoming and everything is well organised, this will help participants to feel at ease and to take part with confidence.

## Giving Instructions

The ability to give clear instructions is crucial. To do this the facilitator must be crystal clear about why the particular activity is being undertaken, the intended outcomes and the steps involved. If not, it is unlikely that they will be able to help others understand effectively! Here are a few tips:

- Before leading a session, 'walk through' the whole programme in your mind and ensure that you have clear, helpful instructions in your mind (or written down) for each step.
- Always give one instruction at a time.
- As far as possible, anticipate and answer people's questions before they are asked (Why? What? How? What if?).
- Check that everyone has understood. This is done by asking, but also by observing facial expressions and body language.
- If an activity does not proceed as intended, move quickly to ensure that it does. If confusion or misunderstanding is widespread don't hesitate to call for the whole group's attention again. If there is one group or an individual who seem to be stuck or heading in the wrong direction, draw alongside and help – or ensure that one of the facilitation team does.

## Ground rules

It is good practice to agree some basic 'ground rules' during the introductory part of an activity. If several activities are being undertaken, it will be adequate to establish these explicitly during the first activity and then give a gentle reminder at the beginning of others. It is best to develop ground rules in an interactive/participatory way, rather than the facilitator imposing pre-prepared rules. If participants are involved in establishing some ground rules, agreement is developed among the group. However, in facilitating the creation of some ground rules, the facilitator will want to ensure that areas such as the following are included:

- Respect – everyone has a valuable perspective based on their unique set of experiences. We must respect each other's contributions.
- Active listening – not only do we listen to each other, but we listen intently, eagerly, curiously – seeking to understand what the other person is communicating. It is a privilege to listen to another person.
- Everybody should have an opportunity to contribute – if necessary the facilitator may suggest a 'nobody speaks twice until everybody speaks once' principle. If this is used it is important to emphasise that nobody should feel 'put on the spot' or forced to speak when they would rather remain silent. Ensure that people know that they can say 'I have nothing to say at this point' without embarrassment. Group working is generally most effective if only one person in a group speaks at any one time and side conversations are avoided.
- Switch off mobile phones – unless people really need to have them on in case of a possible emergency call, in which case they should put them onto a 'vibration only' mode.

## Making the most of a flip chart

Used well, this simple tool is versatile and effective; used poorly, it can be a source of confusion and frustration. If you are not in the habit of using a flip chart, a little time spent in preparation and practice will be worthwhile. Here are a few tips:

- Check you have marker pens. Different colours are useful. Choose dark, saturated colours. Check they are not drying out and that there is enough paper.
- Position the flip chart to maximise visibility and be ready to move it as necessary.
- Print, don't write. Print large. Be neat. It matters.
- If you find it difficult to maintain horizontal text (there is a tendency to dip towards the end of lines), pre-mark pages with a faint pencil line.
- Use colour consistently, e.g. black as a base colour, red or blue to emphasise key words or annotation.
- When recording feedback, write what people say – not what you wanted them to say! If summarising, check with the person that you are being faithful to their contribution.
- Use pictures. You don't need to be an artist and you can always pre-prepare. Use pencil to give yourself invisible hints.
- You will sometimes want to refer back to flip chart pages, so have the means to display pages on a wall, on a board or, with a small group, on the floor.

## The dynamics of discussion

Usually, having prepared carefully and employed the skills outlined above, the scene is set for conversations that are characterised by a genuine curiosity about other people's perspectives. This fosters a desire to listen, learn and discern together. However, occasionally, discussion can become cynical, adversarial, uncompromising or critical. At such times, a grasp of group dynamics and the nature of conversation can help facilitators to understand the processes at work and nurture healthy and productive discussions.

By studying the social interactions between people it has been observed that people operate in what some psychologists refer to as different 'ego states' – child, parent or adult. Most people will move from one to another during their interactions with others, and do so quite unconsciously, but there are clues in the language that they use to what ego state someone is in.[1]

The Parent ego state often assumes responsibility for ensuring the outcome of interactions, therefore the manner and language employed can be critical and demanding (Critical Parent), or protective and sympathetic (Nurturing Parent).

The Child ego state, lacking a sense of control, often seeks to achieve its ends by behaviour designed to elicit a favourable response in Parents. This can either be manipulative and appeasing (Adapted Child) or playful, impulsive and fun-loving (Free or Natural Child).

The Adult ego state avoids manipulation, and is characterised by assertive behaviour and language, rather than either passive or aggressive.

There are three main types of interaction between people, as shown in the diagram.

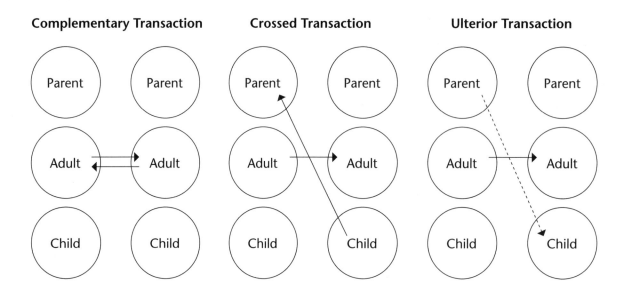

*Complementary transactions* are between persons in the same ego state: parent–parent, adult–adult or child–child. The responses are as expected and there is no resulting conflict.

*Crossed transaction* occurs when one person is in one ego state, and the other is in a different one: for example, adult–child, parent–child. These interactions can be manipulative. For instance, to manipulate someone into yielding to us, we might adopt the critical parent state, becoming demanding and critical, or the adapted child who seeks to bring out the nurturing parent in the other by evoking sympathy.

*Ulterior transactions* occur when the verbal communication and non-verbal communication (tone, expression and body language) are at odds: that is, the words used may be 'adult', but the body language might be that of the critical parent (shouting, pointing, etc.). When the verbal and the non-verbal communication contradict one another, people will instinctively believe the non-verbal – this is what will leave the lasting impact.

As you can imagine, when facilitating a group discussion, complementary adult–adult transactions are more likely to result in positive, creative discussion. While it is appropriate at times in any discussion to acknowledge how people are feeling, an adult to adult transaction strives to de-emphasise the emotional and remain objective. It focuses on moving forward and finding solutions, rather than seeking to assign blame. Questions, rather than outright rejection of another viewpoint, ensure that people feel they have been heard, and that their concerns genuinely matter.

A facilitator can find clues in the language that participants use, and can gently steer the discussion back to an adult–adult dynamic when it strays into crossed or ulterior transactions. In order to do this, it is important that the facilitator remains in the adult ego state. Even when people in the group respond in a parent or child mode, a facilitator can influence the dynamic of the conversation by continuing to communicate as an adult. Although this may seem to create a crossed transaction initially, by persevering it sets a tone in the room that encourages respectful, non-manipulative, solution-focused interactions. Remember too, that if you are using 'adult' words, but your body language is saying something different, then it will be the non-verbal that people will absorb. It is worth persevering with this way of responding until it becomes a habit. Take some time regularly to notice and try to identify what ego state you are in when you are in conversation with others. In a short time you will become familiar with the clues, and be able to respond intentionally, rather than instinctively, when you are facilitating.

# A privilege and a responsibility

People who are involved in facilitating often say that they feel privileged to do so. It is challenging and yet, invariably, encouraging. Guiding a group or congregation through the kind of activities in this book is a serious responsibility, but, by adopting the principles above and preparing prayerfully and carefully, experience has demonstrated that it is almost always a positive experience for all involved. These activities, even the most simple – in fact, especially the most simple – have the potential for profound impact. For some who have used them before you, the effect of using these activities has been transformative – revealing fresh insights, inspiring creative ideas and bold visions, stimulating profound learning and deepening commitment. The resources in your hands have proved themselves to be faith-deepening, vision-inspiring, thought-provoking, community-enriching, relationship-strengthening, confidence-encouraging and discernment-enabling.

# Asking the Right Questions

## Why

We often wonder why discussions or reflections don't quite go according to plan, but it can be the quality of the question that can make or break them. We have all experienced the blunt 'yes' or 'no' to the closed question we asked and then had to try our hardest to resurrect the conversation, but do we pay enough attention to the quality of the open questions that we ask and also to how we frame them? Having a few good questions readily available to spark discussion or get people reflecting can open up learning opportunities or consolidate good learning, ultimately creating a culture of good questioning that leads to better and deeper learning and growing.

When facilitating a group a significant part of your role is to help people find their answers, but it often involves helping them form the right questions. Exploring how to ask for what you need, whether you require information or a dialogue about a complex topic, can avoid frustration and conflict, but questioning and opposing others with the right question allows facilitation of a process of refining, leading to better-quality concepts or content.

## What

What makes an effective or powerful question? There are various types of questions that allow us to do different things. For example, a closed question can shut down conversation, but if you are deliberately looking for a specific answer a more convergent approach is best.

- Could you hear the reading during the service this morning?
- Are we ready to start?

Conversely, open or divergent questions allow for many possible answers without requiring one particular or 'correct' answer. The more open the questioning, the more opportunity for participation and conversation.

- How might we improve our social time after the church service?
- What things help you to pray?

Questions can also be simple or complex. Often a question that is direct and clear allows people to engage more effectively. Questions that are more layered and complex are not necessarily bad, but if there is a degree of explanation, instruction or interpretation involved, this will require more time to think about and to respond appropriately.

- What has made you curious?
- Thinking about all the things we have discussed and explored in our sessions today, are there any issues or important things that we haven't covered that need consideration?

## How

It is important to note how people process the information or concept and formulate answers. Some people like to talk through their answer, processing as they speak with others. Some people like to reflect on their own or internalise until they have formed an opinion or answer. It is a good idea to allow for different learning styles to be explored. Asking questions in different ways, displaying them on a screen or on boards to write on, will allow people to think and express themselves in a variety of ways. While you facilitate conversation or discussion you may wish to vary between asking people to journal/doodle individually, discuss in pairs, converse in small groups, or involve the whole room in discussion.

- How do you feel about …?
- What seemed important or significant from the discussion we have just had?
- When have you experienced…?

## When

Questions can be used effectively to help at different times in our various gatherings. Whether you are starting a meeting, beginning a conference, measuring where people's energy levels are at during a long meeting, or rounding up and coming to the close of a session, a good question can help people focus or widen participation.

Perhaps when you are starting a meeting, asking people to share something that has seemed important from their week can help encourage them to open up and listen. Asking a further question like 'What do you hope to get from this conference?' can help people find common interests or allow them to focus more on their learning and involvement within the session.

- What did you agree with and why?
- What did you disagree with and why?
- How does this resonate or not with your experience?

## Where

There are lots of different situations and styles of gathering that can benefit from well thought out questions. Kirk Sessions or committee meetings, prayer meetings, personal devotions (see 'Asking Questions of Our Day' exercise on page 117), corporate worship or training sessions: each of these scenarios can benefit from raising our curiosity and focusing our thoughts through asking relevant and insightful questions.

## Identifying the wrong question

When facilitating a meeting or discussion, identifying when people are asking the wrong question is as important as asking the right question. Sometimes meetings don't go to plan. Sometimes decisions can't be made or people get bogged down with a particular issue and the answers that we need seem unobtainable and it isn't always obvious why. If you keep getting the same answers, perhaps it is time to change the question! Holding to the purpose of the meeting and ensuring that time, energy and creativity are not directed at answering questions that the particular group have no influence over is essential.

It can be discouraging for a facilitator when things don't quite work or come together or we don't get the answers we thought we would. Keep in mind this is not failure, it is feedback. Any answer given is information. How we then choose to use that information or data is significant. Derailing a conversation or discussion to ask a more searching question to allow things to progress can often be exactly what is needed (see 'The dynamics of discussion' section of 'Facilitation Made Easy' on page xiii). Remaining both objective and curious is key. When discussions lose focus or participants become emotional or argumentative, having questions that can get to the root of the issue or explore why things are triggering responses from certain individuals is invaluable in helping people keep to the purpose of the meeting and refocus on getting constructive answers. Remember, if the question is telling people the answer, it is not a question.

# Section 1

# REFLECTING ON WHOSE WE ARE

# Introduction

'The unconsidered life is not worth living', claimed the Greek philosopher, Socrates. It seems that in ancient Greece the danger of living a superficial and shallow existence was as real and as tragic as it is in the present-day Western world. For much of our lives we operate at an unconscious or subconscious level. Careful consideration and thoughtful reflection are not customary to most of us. In the buzz and bustle of the day-to-day round, conscious contemplation is not the norm.

While we have a remarkable capacity for mind*ful* living, much of life is mind*less*. Like a rudderless raft, rushed onwards by the powerful currents and rapids of a swollen torrent, we are carried along by the flow. Unconsidered living is easy. However, while it may be the default practice, we are called to a deeper and more purposeful reality. An unconsidered life deprives a person of meaning and purpose; a lack of mindful reflection robs our faith of its wonder and transformational power; neglect of contemplation and prayerful consideration stunts Christian growth and renders Christian community cold and lifeless.

As those who seek to follow Jesus Christ and to model our lives on his, we are challenged to live a life of service and compassion, but also to find direction and strength through prayer and reflection. It is undeniable that Jesus was a man of action and yet, again and again, the Gospels recount his patterns of withdrawal and prayer. Although we often find him in the thick of the unrelenting jostle and remorseless demands of crowds, it was his habit to spend time out – consciously in the presence of God and, if possible, away from the demands of ministry. Sometimes he sought this in solitude, sometimes with close friends. When, as was (and is) often the case, finding opportunities for focused prayer and reflection proved challenging, he created possibilities for retreat in inventive ways: sometimes rising before dawn, sometimes taking to the water in a boat, occasionally spending the night on a mountainside (Mark 1:35; 1:45; 3:13; 6:30–2; 6:45–6). Jesus knew the truth that to grow and thrive as God's people requires a faith which is considered and applied.

The Christian life is dynamic and relational. The adventure of faith does not comprise propositions to argue or rules to obey, but rather a relationship with God and with one another. There is good reason why the metaphor of a 'journey' is often employed to describe the experience of the Christian Way. It resonates with our own experience of the ups and downs, the joys and sorrows, the highways and crossroads of life – and it echoes what we know of those who have walked this way before us. Indeed, the Bible is full of journeys, of people on the move. Many of these are physical movements from one place to another; all are journeys through which God accomplishes character makeover and the formation of a people who increasingly reflect his nature. Israel's desert wanderings entailed travel through space and time, but primarily were a journey of Godward transformation. From our view-point, we can see that their route through the desert, to greater understanding and towards more godly character, was unnecessarily long and circuitous. Greater reflection along the way, having the courage and humility to consider their faith and how they were allowing it to direct their path and reorientate their lives towards the Lord, could have saved many miles and considerable distress.

In a culture where faith is often understood to be a private matter and at a time when life is commonly understood in highly individualistic ways, the activities in this section offer some timely and necessary possibilities for personal and corporate contemplation. The exercises in the following pages offer ways to reflect on Scripture and tools to help us consider and articulate our personal experiences of God, his work in our lives and in the world, his faithfulness and provision. Here, too, are valuable means to encourage and enable us to listen to and be enriched by the experiences and perspectives of others. By engaging in these activities with your congregation or group, you will inspire and equip people for the life-long undertaking to: 'Keep your roots deep in him, build your lives on him, and become stronger in your faith, as you were taught' (Col. 2:7, GNB).

# Inspiring Conversations: Using Images to Prompt Thinking and Discussion

## Purpose

To use the power of metaphor and image to help individuals and groups to have conversations or discussions about topics that they might otherwise find difficult.

## Time required

From a few minutes to as long as you wish.

## Resources required

- A set of cards containing random images.[2] It is important to have at least 50 cards and a wide variety of images.
- The only other resource is a carefully worded question (see 'Asking the Right Questions' on page xvi and some examples below).

## Instructions

1 Spread out the cards where they are easily visible. This could, for example, be on a table which people can gather around or on the floor within a circle of chairs. Invite participants to quietly look at the cards while considering a question related to a topic or theme you wish to explore. For example:
   - 'Is there a card here which says something to you about this congregation or group?'
   - 'Is there a card here which says something to you about your experience of prayer?'

3

- 'Is there a card here which says something to you about your experience of this community?'
- Instruct participants not to pick up any cards until asked to do so, as other people in the group may also be drawn to the same card.

2 Gather participants together and ask if someone would be willing to say which card they were drawn to – and why, for them, the image resonated with the question you asked them to consider. Be careful not to put people on the spot. There should be no sense of pressure, but rather an atmosphere of freedom and trust. Simply invite responses.

> *'Having that card in my hand made it easy to say something. Otherwise I think I would have struggled … Fascinating to hear what everyone had to say.'*

## What next?

Depending on the context in which this activity takes place, you may wish to summarise and record what people share and use it as the basis for deeper reflection or discussion. You can also use this activity as an effective icebreaker, helping to encourage people's thinking and sharing ahead of many of the other activities in this book.

# Threefold Portrait of God: Creating a Collage of the Trinity

## Purpose

To enable participants to reflect on their experience of God, and to share that with a wider group, by creating a collage of images relating to each of the three persons of the Trinity.

## Time required

40 minutes–1 hour.

## Resources required

For each small group:

- A large selection of magazines containing colour photographs or illustrations. Ideally, there will be a good selection, representing different interests, and appealing to different groups of people.
- 3 large sheets of paper, size A2 or larger (flip chart paper is ideal).
- Several pairs of scissors.
- Glue sticks.
- 2 or 3 Bibles, different translations if possible.
- 2 or 3 hymn books.
- A selection of coloured marker pens.
- 1 sheet of A4 paper per person.
- 1 pen per person.

# Instructions

1 Prepare the large sheets of paper in advance. On each sheet put the name of one of the persons of the Trinity. Father, Son and Holy Spirit are commonly used, but others may be appropriate, such as Creator, Redeemer and Sustainer, or God, Jesus and Spirit.

2 Ask people to sit in groups at tables equipped with the resources listed above, and explain the purpose of the activity.

3 Invite everyone to reflect on their experience of the first person of the Trinity (Father, Creator, etc.) by looking at the images in the magazines, or by using the imagery in the Bible, or in the words of hymns for inspiration.

4 Encourage people to add words or images to the first large sheet. These can be written or drawn, or be words or images cut from the magazines and stuck to the sheet using the glue stick.

5 Repeat steps 4 and 5 for each of the other two persons of the Trinity.

6 When everyone has had a chance to contribute, lay out the three sheets, and invite people to look at them. Give people a few minutes of quiet to do this.

7 Invite people to share their responses. It may help to prompt the discussion with some simple questions, such as: What stands out to you? Is there anything that you feel drawn to? Is there anything there which jars? What questions does this raise for you about God?

8 When there is a sense that the discussion is slowing down, and everyone has had the opportunity to contribute, invite people to sit quietly and reflect. Make paper and pens available at this point, for people to spend a few minutes in personal journaling, if they wish.

# Variations

• If there is time after step 8, encourage people to look at the collages made by other groups.
• For a quicker exercise, use only one sheet per group, and reflect just on images of 'God'.

# What's in a Name?
# Exploring Biblical Names of God

## Purpose

To enable participants to reflect on their experience of how God has been revealed to them, and to share that with a wider group, by looking at some of the names of God in the Bible.

In understanding better *whose* they are, God's people can enrich the experience of discipleship.

## Time required

About 1 hour.

## Resources required

- Worksheet for each participant with around 8–10 different names of God. There are three sample lists to choose from at the end of the exercise, or you can create your own.
- At least 1 Bible per group. If possible, try to provide a variety of translations for each group.
- 1 pen per person.
- Paper to make notes on.

## Facilitator notes

These days, people choose names for their children for all sorts of reasons – including to honour a family member or a personal hero. Some expectant parents will research the meaning of names before choosing something suitable. Perhaps they will choose a name primarily because it is aesthetically pleasing.

We don't normally expect that a person's name will reveal much about their character or nature, but in the world of the Bible names revealed a great deal. To know someone's name was to know something about them. This is as true for God as for any of the others who populate the pages of Scripture. Throughout the Bible, God has been revealed to people in a variety of ways, and by a variety of names, including Almighty, Lord, Father, the Good Shepherd. People came to understand different aspects of God's character as they had the need to know God in a new way. It is reasonable to assume that God continues to be revealed in specific ways to different people at different times. How we see God affects the stories we tell about our faith, how we serve, and it shapes our values and priorities. Exploring how our understanding of God is shared with, or differs from, our neighbours can help us to be more understanding of others' priorities and vision for the Church.

Where there is a strong sense that God is being revealed in a particular way to a congregation or group, it can provide insights into the worship, ministry and mission of the church.

## Instructions

1 Set up the room in advance, with tables for groups. Make sure there are Bibles, pens and paper on each table.

2 As a short connecting-up exercise, invite people to share their names with their group, including any embarrassing middle names, and explain how they came to be given them.

3 Explain the purpose of the activity, and you may want to provide some of the information in the facilitator's notes.

4 Distribute a worksheet to each person. You can create your own, or choose from one of the worksheets at the end of this exercise: Names of God in the Old Testament, Names of God in the New Testament, or Names for Jesus in Scripture. Allow 6–8 minutes for this.

5 In groups, ask everyone to look at the names in the first column, and share their first impressions. What is familiar – are there any they particularly warm to? Are there any they hadn't heard before? Do any seem strange, or incongruous? Allow 5 minutes.

6 Invite the groups to work their way through the list again, this time reading the Scripture references in the Bible, and to note what strikes them in the 'Comments' column on their worksheet. Does the context of Scripture cast new light on any of them? If this was how God had chosen to be revealed, how would they feel – what would be their reaction?

7 Invite people to share their own impressions. Do they feel God wants to be known in a new or different way? Are they being reminded of something they had forgotten about God?

8 When there is a sense that the discussion is slowing down, and everyone has had the opportunity to contribute, invite people to sit quietly and reflect. Some people may want to make use of the available paper and pens for personal journaling at this point.

# Worksheet: Names of God in the Old Testament

| | Name | Scripture References | Notes |
|---|---|---|---|
| 1 | Creator (*Elohim*) | Gen. 14:19 Isa. 27:12, 40:28 | |
| 2 | Lord, Master (*Adonai*) | Ps. 16:1–2, 114:7–8, 135:5–6 Lam. 2:1–7 | |
| 3 | LORD, I AM (*Yahweh/(YHWH)*) | Exod. 3:13–15 | |
| 4 | Almighty | Job 6:4, 11:7–9 Isa. 13:4, 6, 14:27 | |
| 5 | Spirit | Gen. 1:1–2 Judg. 6:33–4 Neh. 9:30 | |
| 6 | God who sees me (*El Roi*) | Gen. 16:13 | |
| 7 | The Lord will Provide (*Yahweh Jireh*) | Gen. 22:9–14 | |
| 8 | Everlasting God (*El Olam*) | Gen. 21:32–3 | |
| 9 | The Lord my Shepherd (*Yahweh Roi*) | Ps. 23:1–4 Isa. 40:11 | |
| 10 | The Lord is Peace (*Yahweh Shalom*) | Judg. 6:22–4 | |

# Worksheet: Names of God in the New Testament

| | Name | Scripture References | Notes |
|---|---|---|---|
| 1 | The Word | John 1:1–3, 14 | |
| 2 | Father | Matt. 6:6–14<br>Luke 11:9–13<br>John 10: 28–30 | |
| 3 | God (*Theos*) | John 1:1–2,18, 20:28<br>Rom. 8:38–9, 9:5 | |
| 4 | Creator | Rom. 1:25<br>1 Peter 4:19 | |
| 5 | Spirit | Luke 1:35<br>John 4:24<br>Acts 2:4–5<br>Rom. 8:5 | |
| 6 | Living One /<br>Living God | 2 Cor. 6:16<br>Rev. 1:18, 7:2 | |
| 7 | Comforter / Helper | John 14:26 | |
| 8 | Good Shepherd | John 10:11–14<br>Heb. 13:20–1 | |
| 9 | God with us<br>(*Immanuel*) | Matt. 1:23 | |
| 10 | Judge | Heb. 12:22–4<br>James 4:12, 5:9 | |

# Worksheet: Names for Jesus in Scripture

| | Name | Scripture References | Notes |
|---|---|---|---|
| 1 | The Word | John 1:1–3, 14<br>Rev. 19:13 | |
| 2 | God with us –<br>(*Immanuel*) | Isa. 7:14<br>Matt. 1:23 | |
| 3 | Lord<br>(*Kurios*) | Rom. 10:9 | |
| 4 | Alpha and Omega | Rev. 1:8, 21:6, 22:13 | |
| 5 | Messiah / Christ<br>(the anointed one) | Matt. 22:42, 26:63–4<br>Mark 8:27–9, 14:61<br>John 1:15–17<br>1 Tim. 1:15–16, 6:14–15 | |
| 6 | King of Kings | 1 Tim. 6:15–16<br>Rev. 19:16 | |
| 7 | Servant | Isa. 53:11<br>Phil. 2:5–8 | |
| 8 | Lamb of God | John 1:29<br>1 Cor. 5:7<br>Rev. 5:12 | |
| 9 | Light of the World | John 1:6–9, 8:12, 9:5 | |
| 10 | Rabboni / Rabbi<br>(teacher) | John 1:38, 6:25 | |

# Finding Yourself in the Psalms: Using Scripture to Inspire and Guide Reflection

## Purpose

To enable prayerful reflection and the creation of a written response by using the Psalms as a source of inspiration.

## Time required

90 minutes.

## Resources required

- Each participant needs a Bible, notebook and pen.
- For most of the activity people will be sat at a table, but it is preferable to have also a circle of chairs for gathering at the beginning and for sharing feedback at the end.
- A flip chart with some examples of Psalms that relate to particular situations, as follows:
  - When we feel we are in a battle: Psalm 71
  - Dealing with worry or fear: Psalm 46 or 91
  - Confronting doubt: Psalm 22
  - Feeling downcast: Psalm 42, 43 or 77
  - In need of forgiveness: Psalm 32
  - The power of praise: Psalm 145
  - The wonder of it all: Psalm 139
  - Confused? In need of wisdom? Psalm 90
  - A study in happiness: Psalm 126
  - Mid-life or contemplating old age: Psalm 71

– When you've blown it in a big way: Psalm 51
You may want to add your own examples.

## Instructions

1 Sitting in a circle, begin with an inspiring introduction to the Psalms. Something along these lines, perhaps:

> 'It is amazing what people collect. Items of no obvious cash value can be of immense importance to enthusiasts. While those who don't share their passion may fail to see the point, sometimes a committed few have been responsible for preserving invaluable collections for future generations. For example, we should be immeasurably grateful that among our ancient forefathers in faith there were some who collected Hebrew poetry. They collected these poems together into books. Some were poems of lament; others were outpourings of thanksgiving; many were hymns, composed to be sung in communal gatherings of worship, remembrance and celebration. We should be grateful too that, more than five centuries before the birth of Jesus Christ, someone had the vision to collect the collections. In doing so they compiled what became one of the most cherished books of the Bible, the Psalms.'

> 'Despite their ancient origins, the Psalms speak to us. They speak of our almighty creator and sustainer. They also give us a language with which to speak with him. So, while the Psalms contain words *from* God and *about* God, they also include words *to* God. They give us a vocabulary of praise, grief, doubt, trust, anger, thanksgiving and much more.'

> *'It has encouraged me to think more creatively about prayer and how to encourage others to pray ... Through praying through a psalm and working on my own I understood and was able to put into perspective what was happening around me for a while but hadn't had time to digest previously.'*

2 Invite people to 'be still' and become conscious of God's presence using the following or similar instructions:

- 'Close the eyes. Relax the body. Starting from head and moving towards the toes, gradually move the focus of attention to different parts of the body and consciously relax each area. Breathe slowly and deeply.'

While giving participants time to do this, remind them of God's presence:

- 'Be still, and know that I am God' (Ps. 46:10).
- 'The LORD is near to all who call on him, to all who call on him in truth' (Ps. 145:18).
- 'Relax the mind. Gently but firmly let go of cares, concerns, and anxieties. Hand things over to God.'
- 'Cast all your anxiety on him because he cares for you' (1 Peter 5:7).
- 'Let the emotions settle too. Think about God's love: unconditional, unchanging and undeserved. Allow yourself to bask in this love, as if sunbathing. Let God's love surround you and fill you.'

3 Invite people to reflect quietly and honestly before God regarding their present feelings/emotions or situation. This might be about where they are at today or it might be more generally about how they are 'these days' or their circumstances. Say something along the lines of: 'Abraham Lincoln was probably right when he said, "You can fool all the people some of the time, and some of the people all the time, but you can't fool all the people all the time." However, when it comes to prayer – conversation with our loving God – we do well to remember God's omniscience; God is all-knowing. The apostles knew it: "Lord, you know everyone's heart" (Acts 1:24).'

4 After some time reflecting on this quietly, invite people to record in their notebook what has come to mind. This could take the form of thanksgiving, a cry of pain, an expression of confusion or frustration, a sense of wonder or guilt … or anything.

5 Drawing attention to the flip chart, ask whether there is a Psalm there that speaks to people's situation – or whether there is another Psalm that has spoken to them recently or in the past or is special to them.

6 Ask participants to go to one of the tables, maintain silence and to read the Psalm slowly and prayerfully two or three times, recording ways in which this Psalm speaks to them and/or the thoughts and feelings it arouses.

7 Invite participants to recall a time or times when God has helped them in the past. Ask them to write down their understanding of who God is and how God helps them – possibly using one or some of the many names used in the Bible for God or for Jesus. Draw attention to a flip chart or to a worksheet with some examples.

8 Ask participants to review their notes and to draw together their thoughts in a short Psalm of their own along the following lines:
   • An honest expression of current situation or feelings.
   • Recollection of a time when God has helped.
   • Express who God is to you/for you (perhaps using one of the 'names of God').
   • Invite God to work in you and your situation.

9 Gather again in the circle. Invite feedback, being careful to explain that the things that some people have written will be personal and not for sharing, but that others may feel that they have an encouragement to share or may wish to give feedback about the whole exercise. Close with a prayer and blessing.

# Body Image:
# Who is Christ for Us Today?

## Purpose

To enable participants to reflect on their experience of how Christ is revealing himself to them, not just through history and Scripture, but as a living person today. The Church is called to be the body of Christ; understanding who Jesus Christ is today will influence what that body will be like.

## Time required

About 1 hour.

## Resources required

- 1 copy of the 'Body Image' worksheet for each participant. (If images would be helpful for section (b), a quick search on the internet will give a number of useful results.)
- 1 pen for each participant.
- 1 Bible for each small group.

## Facilitator notes

The teaching of Jesus was always relevant and meaningful to his audience. He used metaphors and analogies that would have struck powerful chords with those who heard them, to help him reinforce a particular point. Nearly twenty centuries later, from the cell where he had been imprisoned by the Nazis, theologian Dietrich Bonhoeffer continued to think and write about his faith. In one of the letters he wrote from his prison, he urged his readers to consider the importance of regarding Jesus not just as a historical, or even biblical character, but as a living person in the world today. 'Who is Christ really for us today?' he thought was one of the most important questions we can ask, and theologians continue to ask it more than 70 years after his death. It is a question whose answer shapes who the body of Christ, and its members, will be as we live in our own time and culture.

## Instructions

1  Set up the room in advance, with tables for groups. Make sure there are Bibles, pens and copies of the worksheet on each table.

2  As a short connecting-up exercise, invite people to think of the animal that they most resemble, and why, and to share this with their neighbour for a few minutes.

3  Explain that metaphors are useful for highlighting a particular aspect of a person or thing. The Bible uses metaphors extensively to make its meaning clear and relevant to its audience at that time, and we can continue to use metaphors that make sense in our own context. You may want to add some of the information in the facilitator's notes.

4  For about 15 minutes, invite people to look at the first section of the worksheet in their groups – the 'I am' sayings of Jesus from John's gospel. Discuss what point Jesus might be making with each of these particular metaphors.

5  Since biblical times, societies have used other metaphors for Jesus – some examples are listed in the second part of the worksheet. Invite the groups to spend some time listing others that they are aware of. Allow about 7 or 8 minutes for this. Take 1–2 minutes to take feedback from the groups.

6  Ask the groups to consider the question 'Who is Christ for us today?' It may be one of the names already mentioned, or something new. Some useful prompt questions for the discussion are:
   • What has the Church been in danger of forgetting about Christ?
   • What are the needs in our communities – what is it about Christ that may be a blessing to them?
   • Is there a metaphor for Christ which would be helpful today that remains faithful to Scripture?

   There is space on the worksheet, section (c) for their notes. Allow 15 minutes for this.

7  The Bible uses the metaphor 'the body of Christ' to describe the Church. If our neighbours are to meet Jesus through the life of his followers, what are the implications for us? Are there things we need to change, do more of, or stop altogether? Allow 10 minutes for this.

# Worksheet: Body Image

## (a) Metaphors Jesus used for himself in the Gospel of John

|   | Metaphor | Scripture References | Notes |
|---|----------|---------------------|-------|
| 1 | Bread of life | John 6:35 | |
| 2 | Light of the world | John 8:12 | |
| 3 | The door | John 10:9 | |
| 4 | The good shepherd | John 10:11 | |
| 5 | The resurrection and the life | John 11:25–6 | |
| 6 | The way, and the truth, and the life | John 14:6 | |
| 7 | The true vine | John 15:1 | |

## (b) Examples of Cultural Metaphors for Christ

|   | Metaphor | Cultural Reference | Notes |
|---|----------|-------------------|-------|
| 8 | Shepherd | Images of Orpheus carrying a lamb were appropriated by early Christians, persecuted and in need of a protector. Images still remain on the walls of the Roman catacombs. | |
| 9 | Pantocrator/ ruler | As Christianity became legitimised in the Roman and Byzantine empires, the image of an Emperor Christ proclaimed the majesty of Christ. | |
| 10 | Rebel leader | In Latin America in the twentieth century, Christians needed a saviour who was a political activist, who stood against the corrupt powers of the land. | |

## (c) Who is Christ for us Today?

| Metaphor | Why? | So What? |
|----------|------|----------|
| | | |

# If Faith Was a Football Match: Assessing Our Own Faith Journeys

## Purpose

To help people to reflect on their individual faith journeys, to recognise the value of the journey thus far, and to seek appropriate support in moving forward.

## Time required

About 1 hour.

## Resources required

- 1 instruction sheet (containing descriptions of football match characters) per person (see worksheet).

## Instructions

1 According to the number present, divide the people into small groups.
2 Ensure every person has a copy of the worksheet and read out the scenarios on your own copy. Then explain that they may have approximately 10 minutes to prayerfully consider where they may each 'fit in'. They may believe that they have traits that can be found in more than one character and this is perfectly permissible – there is no instruction to force them into matching just one character.
3 Once this has been done, invite everyone to share their findings among their groups (in confidence). Allow 20–25 minutes for this.

4 Conclude the exercise by conducting a plenary session in which you ask questions that don't necessarily invade any *individual*'s faith journey (some of which may be very personal), but gain a sense of the 'spiritual temperature' of the room.

5 Sample questions may include the following:
- Is there a particular character that is common within your group?
- How broad a range of characters does your group have?
- Is there a character that nobody in the group matches with?
- What (if any) 'spiritual temperature' of the group do you detect from this exercise?

## What next?

Being able to appraise one's 'position' in terms of a faith journey allows for openness to ways forward, but also for acknowledging gifts, together with ideas as to how those gifts may be effectively used.

There are a number of courses available that both help people to go deeper in their faith and to help with discovering or using their gifts. It may be possible to host an 'open evening' where these initiatives can be explored and opportunities taken up.

# Worksheet: If Faith Was a Football Match

All of us are at different stages on our faith journeys and we also have different gifts, talents and experiences. Sometimes it can be difficult to appraise where we 'are at', but perhaps by using the analogy of a football match we may gain some idea of where we are and of how we might relate to others. Please read through the character roles below and try to discover which best matches your current situation.

Please don't take the following character roles literally! They are merely a guide and, indeed, you may find your faith journey fits into more than one of the roles.

### Car park attendant

You are outside the stadium and missing out on all the action, but that's OK. Your job is nevertheless important and you are dedicated to your role and to your colleagues. You love your church and are dependable. You like to stay in the background, so evangelism and teaching are not on your agenda, nor anything to do with leading in worship, but you will always support such work. You are keen to back any charitable cause, but personal Bible study and prayer times are not regular commitments.

### Head of ground staff

You are a passionate supporter of the team and the club. You get on well with just about everyone and enjoy watching the matches. However, as you watch from the players' tunnel, you wince every time a tough tackle goes in and a clod of turf shoots up from the pitch! You care a lot about sacred spaces and their spiritual significance. You love to worship in the beauty of the main sanctuary, but not in other, less 'appropriate' places. You are charitable, but shy away from talking about your faith. You like to live out your Christian faith as a witness to others, but not to discuss it much. You are, however, happy to talk about your church, along with its activity and, in particular, topics that concern the church building.

### Season ticket holder

You are a passionate supporter of your team and never miss a home match. You are a great encourager and spur on your fellow believers in their own faith journeys. You don't commit to any specific task such as youth work or leading a house group, but you never miss a Sunday service. You recognise the gifts in others, but perhaps don't realise what gifts you have yourself. As a result, you rarely get 'stuck in' with commitments outside Sundays. You are comfortable praying alone and will often pick up your Bible, but tend to shy away from doing so with others.

### On the substitute's bench

You are watching a lot of gifted people running all over the pitch and earning praise for their efforts. You are a bit frustrated as the game wears on, fearing you may never get to kick the ball at all. You are gifted, but at the moment, there does not seem to be an opportunity for you to exercise those gifts. You are a team player and enjoy fellowship and you are comfortable praying with others. You are keen to serve God and his church, but the next steps on your faith journey seem unclear. It is, perhaps, up to others in more senior positions (under authority from the coach) to prompt you into action, recognising how your skills and gifts can best be used and then pointing you in the right direction.

### On the pitch, playing!

You are busy, getting stuck in to the task of defeating the opposition. You appreciate all the backing you are getting from supporters – from those on the bench and from fellow team members. You feel uplifted by the prayers of others as you eagerly engage with missional work. You love being at the 'sharp end' of church activity and get a lot of energy from doing so. You delve into books and have a good Bible knowledge. You are very comfortable at praying with others, but get frustrated by such a lot of fellow believers who appear not to. Your enthusiasm is obvious, but such busyness does not allow you much time and space to be alone with the Lord and be able to reflect and pray deeply. This is compounded by the fact that few others are stepping forward to help and so you feel you are the only person doing a considerable number of tasks.

### And the coach?

The coach or manager is, of course, the Holy Spirit. The coach's support is vital in helping us move along the journey from being mere outsiders or 'spectators' to getting fully engaged with following Jesus.

# Reading Between the Lines:
# The Practice of Divine Reading

## Purpose

To help people prayerfully read and interact with text, whether Bible or newspaper.

Lectio Divina or 'Divine Reading' is an ancient practice of slow, contemplative reading and praying of the Bible. As we spend time in the presence of God reading through the text, we are invited to listen for the *still small voice* of God. Part of the process is cultivating the ability to listen deeply. This helps us to see beyond our first impressions or even our second impression and move past any judgements or prejudices that may colour thought as we read. As we continue to read, the instruction is to be gently guided, surprised and transformed by the Holy Spirit as we let prayer rise up within us.

The practice of Visio Divina or the 'Divine Seeing' is the activity of interacting with an image, icon or work of art and allowing the same process of listening for God's voice and being attentive to the prayers that rise within us.

Karl Barth is often quoted as saying something along the lines of 'One must hold a Bible in one hand and a newspaper in the other.' The idea of having a context for our prayers, preaching and practice is by no means a new one, but perhaps applying the principles and practice of Lectio Divina to our newspapers may seem novel to some. As we read of various events in our newspapers and media, discovering the layers of the story, understanding the events depicted and hearing of the people affected gives us opportunity to engage with these things in a prayerful way. Applying the deeper reading and listening of these ancient practices of Lectio Divina allows us to see and hear where God is in the midst of current events and allows us to become prayerfully involved in these stories, perhaps prompting us to action, advocacy or empathy.

## Time required

30 minutes–1 hour.

*If participants are unfamiliar with the practice of 'Lectio Divina' you may wish to guide them through a short version using a particular Scripture passage first.*

## Resources required

- Bibles (especially if you are leading a short 'Lectio Divina' first).
- Newspapers or excerpt from a newspaper for all to use as the reading. Once people are more skilled with the process of deeper reading and listening, having different newspapers available will provide variety and opportunity for many different prayers, but for the first few times, focusing on a particular story will allow people to engage and not become distracted and merely read the paper.

## Instructions

Find out from people their experience of 'Lectio Divina'. Perhaps a short sentence from each of the participants about this will act as a good way of connecting the group. Depending on the experience of the group, the following methodology may be applied to Scripture passages or newspaper excerpts.

### 1 Preparation

Settle into the space. Take time to become aware of your surroundings. Ask God to enter into this time of prayer with you. Ask God to speak to you through the reading.

### 2 Lectio (Reading)

Take time to read through the text (either Bible or newspaper, depending on the experience of the participants).
*You may wish to have someone read the passage aloud or include several voices in a repeated reading before asking people to read the text quietly for themselves.*
You are invited to read the text slowly and carefully, not rush ahead in the reading, and to pay attention to what is happening to you as you read.
*Invite people to rest for a moment.*

### 3 Meditatio (Meditation)

Begin to read again and let yourself be led. Ask the Holy Spirit to speak as you read through the text once more. Let yourself be guided to particular details. As your awareness of particular details grows, allow yourself to consider these particular details and feel them more deeply.

*Invite people to rest for a moment, holding on to the particular things stirring in you.*

### 4 Oratio (Prayer)

Let the things you are holding onto form prayers. Let them naturally arise as you react to characters in the story, specific events or emotions.

*Invite people to rest for a few moments.*

### 5 Contemplatio (Contemplation)

Spend time considering what God is saying to you through the reading and the prayers that formed in you.

How will you respond?

You may wish to note your thoughts in a journal for a few moments and capture what feels valuable and important for you to take away from this time.

## Closing the session

Asking people to share around the room may be difficult for some at this point, as they may still be processing their thoughts or feelings stirred by their experience. It may be better to have some refreshments and invite people to informally chat about their experience for a short time.

Perhaps after this you can get a consensus from the group as to whether capturing their thoughts, feelings or prayers in a more formal conversation would be valuable.

# Symbols from the North: Engaging with the Bible

## Purpose

To help create a 'level playing field' as people engage with the Bible and express their understanding of a passage.

This activity opens up the leadership/facilitation of the group since the way to engage with what the group is looking at is pre-set, as are the questions asked. So the leader needs minimal preparation.

The activity is based on the 'Swedish Method' of Bible study, which became popular in student work in the 1970s. In this variation five symbols are used:

- An arrow pointing up ( ↑ ). This represents 'Something which stands out for you concerning God'.
- An arrow pointing horizontally ( → ). This represents 'Something which stands out for you concerning people (yourself/church community/society etc.)'.
- A star ( ☆ ). This represents 'Something new or re-emphasised'.
- A question mark (?). This represents 'Something to ask or explore further'.
- An exclamation mark (!). This represents 'Something to do'.

In order to complete the activity in reasonable time the group should be small in number.

## Time required

About 60–90 minutes, depending on the size of the group.

## Resources required

- 1 Bible for each person.
- 1 pen for each person.
- Either paper to write on or pre-printed sheets of paper: that is, paper with the symbols printed on and spaces left for writing responses below each symbol.

## Instructions

> 'This approach really helped people contribute to the discussion.'

1 Explain that you want people to share what impacts them from the Bible passage which the group is looking at, and that they are going to do this by using five symbols (see section on 'Purpose').

2 Hand out pens and paper, and pre-printed sheets (if using them).

3 Explain what each symbol means or, if they are not pre-printed, ask people to draw the symbols on their blank sheet of paper, leaving sufficient space after each symbol for their response.

4 Pray.

5 Read the Bible passage together.

6 Give people about 5–10 minutes to fill in the sheet (emphasise that there is no compulsion to fill out each section if it is not appropriate to do so).

7 Ask each person in turn to share their response to symbol one (people must feel free not to share their thoughts if these are too personal). Discuss as appropriate.

8 Repeat the process for each of the other four symbols (be careful about timing).

9 Ask what picture has been built up? Might this picture relate to the group or the wider church community and its mission as well as to each individual?

10 Pray.

## What next?

Encourage members of the group, particularly those who haven't had much experience in leading a group discussion, to lead future Bible engagement times using this method.

## Ideas for visuals

See 'Purpose' section above.

# Head, Heart and Hands: A 'Whole-Person' Bible Engagement

## Purpose

To give a quick and simple way for people to express what most strikes them from a passage of the Bible. The response utilises rationality, emotion and action to develop discipleship.

This activity can be done individually and then shared with the group, or as a group exercise.

Three words (or symbols representing the words) are used:

- Head: What idea catches your imagination/intrigues you? Have you any questions? What do you want to think about more?
- Heart: What touches your emotions?
- Hands: So what: what should you now do?

## Time required

About 60–90 minutes.

## Resources required

- 1 Bible for each person.
- Pen and paper.
- Flip chart and markers if a group exercise.

# Instructions

*'Engages the whole person.'*

1 Explain to people that you want them to share what impacts them most from the piece of the Bible they are looking at.
2 They are going to do this by using three symbols.
3 If initially an individual activity, hand out pens/paper/pre-printed sheets. If a plenary group session, use a flip chart to record comments.
4 Explain what each symbol means or, if not pre-printed, ask people to draw the symbols on the blank sheet of paper, leaving sufficient space after each symbol for their response.
5 Pray.
6 Read the passage together.
7 If initially an individual exercise, give people about 3–5 minutes to fill in the sheet. Then ask each person (in 1–2 minutes), in turn, to share their response to symbol one. Note comments on a flip chart and discuss as appropriate.
8 Repeat the process for the other two symbols (be careful about timing).
9 If the activity is a group one from the beginning ask people to respond to symbol one. This could be done by going round the group one-by-one or by having an 'open' response. Record comments on flip chart and discuss as appropriate.
10 Repeat the process for the other two symbols.
11 Pray.

# What next?

If common themes appear this may form the basis for a future conversation about how God may be guiding the church community as a whole, or a particular group within it.

# Ideas for visuals

Use three simple graphics (either pre-printed or hand drawn):

- Head
- Heart
- Hand

# Many Rooms:
# 'Whole-Life' Discipleship

## Purpose

To help us consider how 'Whole-life' is our discipleship. Normally it is used for individual reflection, but it could be adopted for reflection on the life of a church community.

## Time required

The time required will vary, depending on whether this is an exercise for personal or church community reflection, or both.

As there would be no feedback time after personal reflection, 30 minutes would be sufficient, though the leader, being sensitive to the specific context, may want to extend this.

If it is, or includes, a reflection on the life of the church community, this should entail feedback, which will extend the time. Allow 10 minutes for reflection on the church community, 1–2 minutes for each person to feed back and then 15–30 minutes for a conversation based on the feedback. The leader needs to think carefully about the timing and how this may limit the maximum size of the group if there is to be feedback. There is no lower or upper limit on numbers for personal reflection.

## Resources required

- A setting which is free from distractions, particularly noise.
- Bibles to which people can refer.
- Pens and paper for people to make personal notes (or notes to be shared if reflecting on church community).
- Flip chart and pens if there is to be feedback.

# Instructions

Decide whether the reflection for the group will be personal, church community, or both. The following points will assume personal reflection, but are easily adopted for reflecting upon the church community.

1 Explain to the group that you want them to imagine their life as a house with many rooms and corridors. Each room and corridor represents an aspect of their life. The house was initially dark, but now there are lights on, illuminating some rooms and corridors; some doors are open. For those rooms with windows, the shutters and curtains have been pulled back and the windows have been opened. Other rooms are shut up and closed, some of them are locked.

2 Explain that the illuminated, open rooms represent those parts of our life where the light of Christ reigns, where the wind of the Holy Spirit blows. The darkened rooms are where we do our best to keep Jesus out.

3 Ask the group to:

   a Close their eyes

   b Imagine a house; take time to discover what it is like: style, size, number of storeys, number of outside doors, basement, attic, décor, etc.

   c Enter by the front door; what do you see?

   d Move into the rooms

      i Which are open and lit up; where are they in the house?

      ii What do these represent in your life?

      iii Take time to enjoy being in these rooms; why are these rooms illuminated and open?

   e Now begin to explore the rest of the house.

      i What are the corridors like and what do they represent?

      ii Where are the shut rooms?

      iii Are some of them locked?

      iv Do any of the rooms have the door ajar?

      v What do these represent in your life?

      vi Why are some rooms locked, shut, or ajar?

      vii Do you want to open these doors, put on the lights and open the shutters/curtains/windows? Why?

      viii What will help you?

      ix What is hindering or what will hinder you?

      x What are you going to do?

   f Light a candle, which symbolises the Light of Christ and which may, for some, help as a focus during the following time of prayer. Offer this as an option to praying with closed eyes (some may prefer to keep their eyes closed as this will help them focus on the issues that they have identified).

g  Prayer

    i  Individual, silent prayer response.

    ii  'Drawing together' prayer by the person who guided the session.

## What next?

This can be a very intense experience for some and the availability of pastoral follow-up is essential.

If this is part of a longer time together, the group may find it helpful to have a break before further discussion. The leader may sense that a change in the agenda would be appropriate and the freedom to make this should have been agreed/discussed beforehand.

## Ideas for visuals

Some may find a candle helpful to focus upon during the prayer time.

Other visuals should not be used as they may limit an individual's imagination.

# Building up a Picture: Collage Bible Engagement

## Purpose

To give an opportunity to express our understanding of the Bible in a visual way.

Not everyone finds words the easiest way to express what they think, believe or feel. This activity uses images from newspapers and magazines to form a collage and through this enables individuals to express their understanding of a passage from the Bible. For those who are comfortable with words, but perhaps not with images, it allows them:

- to look at something in a fresh way;
- to recognise how those who are not as verbally articulate as they are, may, at times, feel.

## Time required

About 1 hour, though depends on the size of group and if people are working individually, in pairs or in groups. A rule of thumb would be to keep as close as possible to the time of your normal Bible study/discussion time.

## Resources required

- A large and varied stock of newspapers and magazines.
- Large sheets of blank paper.
- Scissors.
- Glue.
- Felt tip pens.
- Bible for each person.

# Instructions

1 Explain to participants that you want them to share what most impacts them from the piece of the Bible being looked at and that they are going to do this by creating a collage using pictures or headlines from magazines and newspapers.
2 Decide together if this will be done individually, in pairs or in small groups (some may have difficulty using scissors, or feel at a creative loss).
3 Pray.
4 Read the passage together.
5 Give people about 20 minutes to create their collage.
6 Give each person, pair or small group 1–2 minutes to describe their picture.
7 Discuss what picture you get when you put together the ideas behind the collages.
8 Pray.

# What next?

If people are comfortable with their ideas being shared with the wider church and community, then the collages could be displayed in a public area in the church. If this were a possibility it could be displayed for two weeks in the area where most people who come to weekday activities would see it and then for two weeks where people who come to weekend activities would see it. A short, explanatory paragraph beside each collage is likely to be helpful. They could also be displayed 'on screen' before or after various gatherings/events.

# Ideas for visuals

Visuals are intrinsic to the activity.

# Section 2
# KNOWING ONE ANOTHER

# Introduction

The headlines were arresting; the claims, astonishing. 'One of the most dramatic medical breakthroughs of recent decades' claimed the report in a national newspaper in 2018. During a three-year period, emergency hospital admissions in surrounding regions increased by 29 per cent, but the study area saw a *decrease* of 17 per cent. If the same intervention could be rolled out across the whole country, it would transform treatment regimes, slash National Health Service expenditure and save lives. It did not involve medication. No surgical procedure was required. In fact no specialist training or equipment was needed.

What the researchers had detected was the incredible power of community. By establishing informal groups and networks, friendships were fostered and isolation reduced. What had been rediscovered was the most ancient and fundamental of truths: 'It is not good for the man to be alone'; 'Two are better than one … If either of them falls down, one can help the other up' (Gen. 2:18; Eccles. 4:9–10). Loneliness, described by Mother Teresa as 'the most terrible poverty', kills. In contrast, community nurtures well-being and, it turns out, boosts the immune system.

From the beginning of his ministry Jesus called together a group of companions. When he sent out his disciples to proclaim and demonstrate a new kind of kingdom, he did not send them alone, but 'two by two'. The fruit of the Holy Spirit coming in power at Pentecost was a radically different kind of community: 'All the believers were together and had everything in common' (Acts 2:44). Drawn together by their faith in Christ, this new society was characterised by self-giving love. As we read on in the enthralling account of the early Church, it is clear that this intense and caring companionship, far from being insular and exclusive, was consistently outward-looking; it was a fellowship in which love of the stranger was promoted and practised with the same enthusiasm as love among brothers and sisters.

As Christians, we aspire to that kind of life-changing fellowship. However, community is not just an outcome of proximity. Living next-door to neighbours does not by itself build the relationships that create and characterise transformative community. Likewise, sitting together in church or regularly attending a particular group is no guarantee of mutual understanding or friendship. Community is built by communication. Excellent communication builds strong relationships and, in turn, healthy communities. Sometimes the way we choreograph worship, or manage meetings, or facilitate fellowship encourages deep sharing and meaningful interaction; at other times discussion is closed down, conversation is stilted and the experience of being with others remains shallow and superficial.

The activities in this section are catalysts for conversation. Here are exercises to help people overcome reticence and enjoy one another. Insights from psychology and sociology can help us better understand and value our differences and promote healthy patterns of communication. For example, 'Generational Theory' explains how the era in which a person was born shapes their view of the world. A basic grasp of its key concepts can develop a fuller appreciation of differences and help recognise the roots of our own and others' perspectives. 'Transactional Analysis' may sound highfaluting and technical, but in fact it provides an accessible and uncomplicated means of enriching our interactions with one another and better understanding the ways in which we and others relate together.

Most exercises in this section are straightforward for facilitators and fun for participants. However, don't be deceived – they have the potential to move knowledge and awareness of one another to a deeper level. They can be used to develop skills in active listening, the benefits of which will go beyond a brief exercise and influence other areas of life. Participants often report a sense of 'privilege' in listening to others and in being listened to with genuine interest. Our congregations and groups will be changed by engaging in these kinds of activities – and invariably for the better.

# Human Bingo:
# Connecting up with Others

## Purpose

To help us get to know one another better, in a fun and informal way.

This exercise works well as a connecting-up exercise, as it gets a group of people talking in a natural, unpressured way. It is highly participative, and works well in a larger group as an alternative to asking everyone to introduce themselves, which can leave people passive and feeling disengaged. It also raises the energy in the room by getting people to move about. It is particularly appropriate for groups who don't know one another well. If there are fewer than twenty in the group it can feel forced or stilted.

## Time required

The time required is determined by the number of people in the group and the number of squares on the bingo card to be completed. The more people to get round, and the more information to find, then the longer the exercise, but 10–15 minutes would be about right for an opening exercise.

## Resources required

- Pre-prepared 'bingo card' for each participant.
- Pen or pencil for each participant.
- A small prize for the winner.

# Instructions

1. Prepare a grid in advance for the bingo card, like the one shown below. It will have to be large enough to allow participants to write in the squares. It should ideally have between 15 and 25 boxes. Determine how much time you want to give to this exercise – remember, more time is required for a larger grid. There does not need to be a match between the number of squares on the grid and the number of participants, although there should never be more squares than participants. If you are not sure how many people will be there, plan conservatively.

2. In each of the boxes type a piece of information which may relate to one of the participants, leaving enough blank space in each square to write a name. The information should be interesting or light-hearted, but nothing which will cause embarrassment or discomfort. If you know some of the participants well, for example if you know that they speak a foreign language, have an unusual pet or play a musical instrument, you may wish to include this. Ensure, however, that there are enough general facts that could apply to several people, for example eye colour or wearing a striped shirt. Try to avoid having facts that no-one is likely to match with.

3. Print enough grids for each participant to have one, and make sure that everyone has a pen.

4. Invite people to move around, and by questioning one another, be able to fill in the grid with names of people who match the facts in each square. It is possible that one individual may be a match for more than one square, but players can only use each name once.

5. The game ends either when the first person completes their grid, or when the allotted time is over. It is unlikely that everyone will complete the grid. If no-one has completed their grid, the winner is the person who has filled in the highest number of squares.

# Variations

This exercise can also be used during longer events, for example, a day conference, or at social events, where the attendees don't know each other well, in order to facilitate conversation in break times and between sessions. The winner is the person who has completed most of the grid by the end of the day.

# Human Bingo

Find as many people as you can. You can only write the name of each person ONCE.

| Someone who speaks German | An artist in their spare time | Used to be in the armed forces | Has more than one pet | Born outside the EU |
|---|---|---|---|---|
| | *Alan* | | | *Maria* |
| Has donated blood more than 50 times | Used to work in a carnival | Someone who is a 'middle child' | Made their own wedding cake | Occasionally is a 'mystery shopper' |
| | *Eric* | | *Graham* | *Ali* |
| Once appeared in a TV soap | Is a science teacher | A badminton coach | Has an international hockey cap | A member of an amateur dramatic club |
| | | *Sonja* | | |
| Has a provisional driving licence | Taught a belly-dancing class | Used to be in a rock band | Has owned more than 30 cars | Allergic to mustard |
| *Norman* | | | | *Lucy* |
| Used to be a rat catcher | Forgot to go to *Time Management* training | Has an allotment | Owns a drum collection | Originally trained as a chef |
| | *Davie P* | | | |

# Desert Island Hymns: Using Songs to Explore Faith

## Purpose

To encourage people to talk about their faith journey or prayer life.

Being asked to talk about these things can at times be a daunting or uncomfortable experience, leaving us feeling vulnerable, or as if we don't have a good enough story. So how do we encourage people to normalise this type of conversation and allow them to become more reflective about their spiritual life?

When we have 'normal' conversations and talk about our recent experiences or passions, we can easily find ourselves journeying deeper into conversations we never thought we would have. Finding a way into a deeper conversation generally happens because of questions or prompts from the other people we are with who are curious about what we are talking about. We can help encourage these deep conversations and empower people to become more reflective about their faith by relating these conversations to more everyday topics and using them as metaphors for the deeper things of life.

What is your favourite song? Why do you like it so much? There are lots of different reasons for having favourite songs, books or films, but what do these things tell us about ourselves? If we were to look at our favourite hymn or worship song, what insights might we gain about our faith? Equally, if we were able to choose any one hymn, song or Scripture passage to describe our faith journey, what might we choose and why?

## Time required

About 1 hour, depending on the number of participants.

# Resources required

Having some images of album covers, film posters and book covers may be useful, but they are not essential.

# Instructions

1 Start by asking people to share very briefly about a song, book, film or TV series that has gripped them recently. This is a 'connecting-up' question, so have them chat for only a few minutes. You may want to do this over tea and coffee so that it feels informal and welcoming.

2 Ask people to take some time to consider some of their favourite hymns or worship songs. Spend around 5 minutes reflecting on this either in silent contemplation or by writing some thoughts or doodling in a journal.

3 Invite people to speak to the person next to them about their favourite songs and ask them to share why they are significant or important.

4 Now ask each of the participants to imagine if they were on a desert island and could only have one hymn or worship song with them, which one would it be and why? You may wish to give participants a few minutes to form their thoughts and then ask them to share with the group. Depending on the group, you might want to ask people to share as they feel led rather than moving around in a particular order.

5 As people share you may wish to help them tease out some deeper insights into the significance of choosing a particular song. For example, if they chose a song that is energetic and uplifting – are they someone who enjoys praising God? Is there something significant about thankfulness that resonates for them? Is this the element within worship that helps them feel closest to God?

6 Close the time together by asking people to share what was valuable about the conversations. You may wish to end by singing a hymn or using the words of a hymn as a closing prayer or blessing.

# The Human Anthology: Sharing Our Stories

## Purpose

To create a climate which is relational, open and honest, through telling our own stories.

This exercise focuses on the things which shape our character and personality, rather than on the jobs or roles which we have. People relate to stories, and they stay in the mind more readily than hard facts or lists of information.

## Time required

Time is, in part, dependent on the size of the group, but to go beyond 60–90 minutes is likely, in most cases, to give diminishing returns.

## Resources required

- A set of 'Story Starters' cards for each group.
- Optional: a timer for each group (people may wish to use their watch or phone; 3 minute egg-timers are inexpensive).

## Instructions

1 Prepare a set of question cards for each group. There should be at least 10 cards to choose from – there should be more cards available than there are people in the group. Each card should be size A6 or A7 (a quarter or an eighth of an A4 sheet) – small enough that there is room to spread them out on a table, but large enough that the font can be easily read. Each card should have one question on it (or a single image). See below for a list of suggestions.

2  To get the most from this exercise try to create a relaxed, informal atmosphere. Comfortable seating, tables, refreshments and nibbles all help.
3  Begin by explaining the purpose of the cards.
4  Invite participants to select a card that reminds them of a story from their own experience.
5  Allow everyone 1–2 minutes to consider the cards. It may be appropriate to read them aloud. Invite someone to start. Don't be put off by silence: a strongly extrovert group will be competing to tell their story first, but introverts will need a little more time to 'process'.
6  At the end of each story, thank the storyteller, and leave space for comments or questions, then move on to the next storyteller. You may wish to use a timer, so that everyone gets sufficient time.
7  When everyone who wants to has shared their story, reflect on what has struck you about the stories. Note that some people may have shared difficult or painful stories, and it may be appropriate to use the time at the end for prayer.

## Hints and suggestions

When looking at the content of the cards, consider the following:

1  Who is in the group? Are they Christians, or people of another or no faith?
2  Check that everyone is able to read the conversation prompt cards. Some people might feel excluded on account of visual impairment, literacy or language barriers. You might want to try using picture or symbol cards, or offer to read them aloud.
3  Read the section 'Asking the Right Questions' on pages 19–21, for advice on creating useful questions. Suggested story starters might include some of the following:
   • What is the biggest risk you have ever taken?
   • Describe a time when your life significantly changed direction.
   • What are you celebrating at the moment?
   • How are you involved in your community?
   • What or who has most inspired your life of discipleship?
   • What has given you greatest satisfaction this year so far?
   • What recent discovery have you made about yourself or God?
   • What advice would you give your younger self?
   • What has been hard to forgive?
   • What is the best decision you have ever made?
   • What is your best memory?
   • What did you want to be when you were five years old?
   • What is the biggest thing you have ever got away with?
   • What are you doing at the moment which gives you a strong sense of purpose?
   • What fills you with awe?
   • When have you encountered God in an unexpected place?

- How do you look after yourself (emotionally, spiritually, mentally, physically)?
- ??? (Have a wildcard there for any topic)

4 It is not intended that every question is answered, or that every person has to share a personal story. Similarly, people are free to share something that relates to none of the cards.

5 The prompts should invite the participant to reveal something about themselves – but not push them to the point where they feel pressured or uncomfortable. So, we might learn about someone's interests, or hobbies, or be introduced to other members of their family in the story, but the person telling the story should remain in complete control of the level of personal disclosure.

6 Don't be afraid of the hard topics – not every card will lead to a story in the group – but it just might. Aim for a mix of light-hearted and more profound.

7 If you are doing this exercise as part of a bigger event, do you want the questions to reflect the overall theme?

# Pop-up Polls:
# Gauging the Opinion of a Group

## Purpose

To quickly determine the spread of opinion on a single question within a group.
  This is useful:

- as a connecting-up exercise.
- for gauging the opinion of a group that has become bogged down in a discussion by taking an opinion poll on the theme of a session, or seeing if the group's opinion has changed in the course of an exercise.

## Time required

5 minutes. (This activity requires people to move around, so be sensitive to those with disabilities who may need assistance or a little more time.)

## Resources required

- Sufficient space for all the participants to line up in a straight line.

# Instructions

1 To use as an icebreaker, ask a single closed question (that is, a question which has a yes/no, agree/disagree answer) and ask people to line up, with those who agree at one end of the line, those who disagree at the other, and the others to position themselves between the two, according to their opinion. This can work well if the question is related to the theme. For example, if the main session is about relationships or communications you might ask, 'Social media is good for relationships – do you agree or disagree?'

2 You may repeat this for several questions, which will emphasise that people are different, and may demonstrate that those who share opinions on one matter may strongly disagree on another.

3 This activity also works as an energiser exercise – like an icebreaker, but specifically used when energy in the room is low (for example, after lunch), to get things moving again.

4 To use as an opinion poll, follow the same process but choose the question(s) with care. If the group are meeting to discuss a sensitive issue, it should be clear that this activity is not a vote on the outcome, but merely a means of assisting the facilitator and participants to be clear on what is being communicated. It is a good way of allowing everyone in the room to express an opinion, not just those who are more confident about being vocal in a group. For example, if the group are working on a vision statement, this exercise can be carried out to determine if the group are satisfied with the vision – if they share it – or if there is still some work to be done. The exercise can be repeated later to see if there is movement towards resolution.

# The Phone Call:
# What Gives Us Energy?

## Purpose

To help us better understand both our own and other people's enthusiasms and gifts and how this might relate to the way we live life and serve others.

This activity gives each person in the group the opportunity to share what they are passionate about. It's important to recognise this about ourselves (and others) as some activities drain energy from us and others give us energy. When we understand this about our life in general, it can help us identify what areas of service we are naturally enthusiastic about and which, in turn, can give us energy (even though they might be very demanding).

## Time required

About 40–60 minutes, depending on the size of the group and how the group wants the conversation to develop.

## Resources required

- Flip chart
- Marker pens.

# Instructions

1 Ask each person to imagine that they have had a busy week and that they are really tired. It's Friday night, tomorrow is going to be another full day and for the first time that week they have settled down to relax … then their phone rings ….

2 Now ask them to imagine two scenarios:

- Scenario One: a friend phones to say that they need your help NOW with something and that it will take all evening. It's the activity that you least like: what is it and how do you feel?
- Scenario Two: a friend, who shares your passion for a particular hobby or interest, phones to say that a unique opportunity has come up that evening to pursue this hobby and they ask you to join them. What is this activity and how do you feel when you get this message?

3 Talk together about Scenario One.

- People must feel free not to disclose the activity, but invite each person to talk about how they would feel in the situation. It is likely that the call, never mind carrying out the activity, would drain whatever energy they felt they had.
- If this is the case, what might this say about the sort of service they should not be involved in? For example, if the friend has asked them to help fill in a detailed Tax Return form, perhaps accounting, book-keeping or administration should be avoided if heart and enthusiasm are to be retained.

4 Talk together about Scenario Two

- Give people time to enthuse about their hobby or interest and to say why they enjoy it so much. It is likely that the call in this scenario would give them energy, which they didn't think they had.
- What might this say about areas of service to which they might be attracted, service which might enthuse them and, in turn, give them the energy for the 'longer haul'?

# What next?

Using the flip chart make a note of the group's areas of interests, what might this say to the group about:

- areas of service or mission?
- the potential development of a fresh expression of church?

If the group has been happy to talk about areas which drain energy, what might this be saying to the group?

# Unwrapping Our Gifts: Exploring Gifts, Talents and Passions

## Purpose

To help individuals to explore and also articulate their gifts and talents, and to enable congregations or groups to recognise and celebrate the breadth and diversity of the gifts and talents present in their members.

The aim of this exercise is to encourage and affirm members of the congregation or group, assuring them that each person's unique combination of abilities and passions has a part to play in the life of the church. It is not intended to be a tool merely to help churches fill up existing duty rotas or perpetuate existing programmes and initiatives. While that may indeed be a helpful outcome, at its best this exercise will suggest what the future work of the church may look like as the life of the church is shaped around the gifts of its people.

This exercise will have greatest impact when it is followed up by the leadership of the church. People will know their gifts are valued when they are given the opportunity to use and develop them in the ministry and mission of the church. Conversely, if we have taken the time to talk about their gifts and talents, but then do nothing with that information, it can have a profoundly demotivating effect and make it harder to engage people in the future.

There is, therefore, a note of caution attached to this activity. Unless you are sure that the leadership have both the intention, and the time, to follow it up, then consider whether it is appropriate to hold this exercise.

## Time required

About 1 hour.

# Resources required

- Worksheet for each participant.
- Pens for each participant.
- Flip chart.
- Marker pens.

# Instructions

1 In advance, agree with the church leadership how the information from this exercise will be used, and make plans for how it will be followed up.

2 Arrange people in groups around tables, and provide everyone with a worksheet and a pen.

3 Explain the purpose of the exercise. Make sure people are aware of how the information will be used. It is important that people know if the information will be seen by others, for example if the worksheets are collected at the end and passed to the church leaders. If the worksheets are not anonymous, you – if not the participants – need to know how the information will be stored and handled, so as to protect privacy and comply with data protection legislation.

4 Work through the worksheet one section at a time. Invite everyone to consider their mental, or intellectual gifts. Invite everyone to complete the first section of the worksheet entitled 'Head'. If people in the group know each other, it can be useful to work in pairs, and to learn how others perceive us. If the group consists of people who don't know anyone, ask everyone to work individually, so that no-one feels excluded. Ensure people understand this is not about educational levels, or qualifications. 'What have you learned from your education, your home life, workplace or hobbies?' is a helpful prompt as people think about this. Older people often carry the collective memories of the community, while younger members will understand more about current technology or pop culture. Encourage people to chat in their groups for a few minutes. Remind people to think much wider than just the things that seem relevant to church – this is about the whole of their lives. Allow 10 minutes for this.

5 Take some feedback from people – encouraging people to share at least one thing from their list. Note these on a flip chart at the front, and hang the completed sheet on a wall or display board where everyone can see it. Invite groups to pray for a few minutes, giving thanks for the wealth of knowledge in the congregation or group. This will take about 10 minutes.

6 Repeat steps 4 and 5 for the second section of the worksheet entitled 'Hands'. This section is about practical abilities. Invite people to reflect on the thing they 'do', and which they feel they do well. This can range from parenting skills, sports coaching, organisational skills, music and preaching, to running a household and a myriad of other things. Recalling all the things that we do in the course of a week will give people a good place to start

their reflection. Again, allow time to give thanks for the abilities in the church. Allow 20 minutes for this.

7 Repeat this process again for the third section of the worksheet entitled 'Heart'. In this section we are looking for what people are passionate about. The danger is that people will write down what they *think* they're passionate about. To mitigate this, invite people to share with others in their groups about a time they had a very strong emotional reaction, and think about what triggered it. Was it joy at the birth of a child, sorrow at seeing the devastation of a natural disaster unfold on the news? Maybe it was anger at war or violence, or pleasure at the first flowers of spring. What was at the root of their reaction – love of family or the natural world, a desire for peace or healing, or a fierce need to protect the vulnerable? Invite people to reflect together and then complete that section of the worksheet. Again, note the feedback on a flip chart, and give thanks for the range of things that the congregation or group cares deeply about.

8 The last section of the sheet brings all of this together. Each person will have a unique list of items on their sheet. This means that there are some things that they can uniquely do in the service of God. Invite people to consider all three sections of their own sheet together. Is there something they would love to see the church engage with, and what might they be able to bring to that? It may be that they are able to get involved with something that the church is already doing, or it may be something completely new. Allow people 10 minutes for this.

9 Invite people to share something of their reflections, if they feel comfortable to do so. Again, record this on a flip chart. Explain to the group how the leadership intend to take this exercise forward, and what the next steps are. You may want to collect in the worksheets, but the flip charts may be sufficient. People may want to take their sheets away with them for personal prayer and consideration. Finish the exercise with prayer.

## What next?

The leadership of the church will want to consider how best to follow this up. It is important to do so reasonably quickly and to honour any timescales given at the end of the session, as the energy and momentum of the exercise will dissipate quickly.

# Worksheet: Unwrapping Our Gifts

**Head**
What knowledge do I have from home, education, work, hobbies and so on?

**Hands**
What skills and abilities do I have?

**Heart**
Think about a time when I had a strong emotional reaction. Why? What does this suggest that I am really passionate about?

**So what?**
Are there abilities or knowledge I would get satisfaction from using or developing in the church?

What do I care about that I want to get involved with or learn more about?

Where can I make a difference?

# Bridging the Gap: Understanding Different Generations

## Purpose

To explore what is behind the 'generation gap' and equip participants to better understand the differing viewpoints of people from different generations.

Current research indicates that it is not enough for us to cater for each generation in our churches, but to encourage intergenerational church, where those from different age groups socialise, serve, learn and worship together. In order to do that, it helps when we understand what makes each generation tick.

Each generation is shaped by the context in which it grew up, leading to different world-views, aspirations, concerns, and developing different strengths and concerns. Better understanding can assist in offering more relevant welcome, hospitality, engagement and opportunities for service, while reducing the likelihood of frustrations coming from misconceptions.

## Time required

About 90 minutes.

## Resources required

- Paper for writing notes.
- 1 pen for each participant.
- 'The Generations at a Glance' worksheet for each participant (see end of exercise).
- Pictures or artefacts relating to each generation (optional).

# Facilitator notes

What is a generation, and why is it important?

It does not simply concern a person's age. A generation is a group in a society that, because of the time and place they grew up in, encounter similar historical events, economic forces, social influences and attitudes. They therefore share a perceived social identity as part of that generation and often share similar beliefs, hopes, anxieties, language and even behaviours. A new generation emerges around every twenty years.

This is, of course, a generalisation. Parenting and upbringing, education, affluence, and local circumstances will also play a great part, but there is enough evidence of similarities to warrant our consideration.

As a generation becomes dominant in society, through attaining leadership and influence in government, industry and the media, its values start to shape the culture, creating the environment that subsequent generations will grow up in.

Why is this important to our churches?

'I will sing of the Lord's great love for ever; with my mouth I will make your faithfulness known through *all generations*.' (Ps. 89:1)

Many Christian congregations or groups in the West are not representative of the communities around them. They tend to be older, and the lack of children and young people is often lamented. It is not just young people who are largely absent, as it is common to find that people under the age of fifty are underrepresented. We are called to make God known in *all* generations. Understanding one another better will help us to do that more meaningfully and relevantly.

At the end of this exercise there is a worksheet which can be given to participants during the exercise, but which may be useful to refer to if the groups need some help or prompting. It is important to emphasise that this is not an attempt to stereotype generations, and the information is not intended to be applied to everyone born in the time frames listed.

# Instructions

1   Arrange people into a minimum of four groups, ideally of varying ages in each. Each group will be discussing just one of the generations.
2   Introduce the subject, using the information in the Facilitator notes, and assign a generation to each group: Builders, Baby Boomers, Generation X, and Generation Y. If you have pictures or objects available, place the ones relevant to each generation on each table.
3   Ask the groups to consider the following questions:
   • What were the events or attitudes that would have been around when this generation was growing up?
   • How might that have affected them?
   • What are they like now?

There will be a natural tendency to reminisce during this exercise, so allow sufficient time. People may want to look at the objects – those more familiar with them can explain them to others in the group. Part of the purpose of the exercise is to deepen intergenerational understanding, but don't allow the groups to get bogged down with the first questions. Gently prompt them to move on to the second and third.

Allow some time for the groups to share their thoughts on the different generations.

4  Distribute the worksheet 'The Generations at a Glance'. Invite participants to consider the following questions in their groups:

- What generations are most represented in your congregation or group? How have their characteristics shaped the church?
- What would enable other generations to contribute their best in the life of the church? (If time is restricted, you might want to ask the groups to focus their discussion on the particular generation they looked at earlier.)
- What generation is least represented in your church? What would be good news to someone of that generation?
- What parts of the life of the church are intergenerational, and what opportunities are there to build on this?

5  Ask the groups to share their thoughts in the wider group.

6  Finish the session with prayer, focusing on God's desire to show his love to all generations.


## Variations

If there is time, reflect on the generation that is currently growing up. What is going on now? What effect might that have? What might that generation come to be called?

# Worksheet: The Generations at a Glance

|  | **Builder** | **Baby Boomer** | **Generation X** | **Generation Y** |
|---|---|---|---|---|
| **Born** | Before 1945 | 1946–1964 | 1965–1984 | 1985–2005 |
| **Defined by** | Scarcity, economic instability, upheaval, loss and separation. | Growth, development, building infrastructure, hope, grand visions. | Instability, changing rulebook, economic collapse, uncertainty, change. | Changing rulebook, economic collapse, uncertainty, change. |
| **Motto** | Work hard – do your duty. | If you've got it, flaunt it. | 'Whatever' | Let's make the world a better place. |
| **Loves** | Security, stability. | Shopping, winning, leading, showing off. | Sharing, being with friends, change, individuality. | Shopping, designer labels, family and friends, the environment, technology. |
| **Hates** | Debt, borrowing, precocious youngsters. | Repaying debt, ageing, powerlessness. | Corporate culture, bossiness, fakes. | Dishonesty, unbalanced lifestyle, flashiness. |
| **Character** | Stoic, reserved, clean-living, courteous. | Talkative, bossy, competitive. | Pragmatic, individualistic, arrogant, risk-taking, spiritual. | Tolerant, honest, caring, optimistic. |
| **Today** | Affluent, work hard in retirement, frugal, friendly to other generations. | Hold the reins of power, legalistic, hardnosed, extravagant, don't consult other generations. | Educated, work to live, thrill seekers, in pain, in therapy, huge capacity for information, over-protective, live for now. | Most educated, pampered, high expectations, expect rewards, questioning, need flexibility. |
| **View of God** | Distant but approachable. | Familiar. We can sense him working through us. | Companion, friend, guide and healer. | Provider and protector. |
| **Church** | Orderly, familiar, restrained. Careful stewardship, focus on Bible teaching, still hold authority in many churches, 'What can I do for God? What can I do for church?' | Professional, high quality, visionary, fast-paced, contemporary, strategic. Scripture seen as guide book. Gaining authority or wrestling Builders for power. | Hates 'corporate' church. Relational, contextual, healing space. Very spiritual. Stifled by bureaucracy. Prefer a team approach, won't fight for power – will just leave. | Many access points, 24/7, multi-media, must be relevant, activist, sacred space, journey of discovery. Need a team approach, will challenge authority. |
| **Hope** | Familiar church format. Traditional, not up for change | Flexibility – need ability to accommodate around life and diaries | Looking for new approaches – wants challenges, available to be hooked – *but* how? | No time for church, sceptical. Voluntary work and community help, charities. Projects that matter. |

# Section 3
# EXPLORING OUR CULTURES

# Introduction

Imagine for a moment that you have travelled to a distant country with a culture radically different to the one in which you live. What might be the things you would notice? For a start, the language may be alien to you – so much so that you simply can't understand when people try to communicate with you. When you speak you find you are either not understood or, sometimes worse, you are *mis*understood. Their social habits may be profoundly different from those you are familiar with, possibly leading to embarrassing misunderstandings. The music may seem like an awful noise to you or you may love it, but the chances are that it will be unusual to your ears. Likewise their art, fashion and decor may appear as strange, weird or even ugly to you. Soon after arriving, you will no doubt discover that the cuisine of this foreign land is another adventure into the unknown. It may be a pleasant surprise or you may struggle to digest it. The sight of a meal that makes the locals drool with eager anticipation may leave you wondering whether this visit was a terrible mistake!

What has this got to do with this book and your group or congregation? Well, like any other group of human beings that gathers together on a regular basis, your group or congregation will have its own 'culture'. Just as a local person in the foreign land you just imagined would find it difficult to see and describe their *own* culture (after all it is simply 'normal' to them), it will be a challenge for you to recognise your own culture.

So why bother? Examining the culture of our group or congregation from time to time is important on a number of levels. First, we need to ensure that the culture we create (often unconsciously) is appropriate for a group or congregation of people who are seeking to build their lives on the good news of Jesus Christ and share his love with others. The New Testament contains many letters to particular congregations and we don't need to read between the lines too much to realise that the writers are often challenging the culture that particular fellowships of Christians have developed. Beliefs, attitudes, relationships, leadership styles, worship practices and many other things that contribute to church culture are put under scrutiny and challenged. Obvious examples include the letters to seven different congregations that are recorded in the second and third chapters of Revelation. Practices that have become 'normal' are challenged and these churches are called upon to change their culture in significant ways.

Second, another important reason for giving careful attention to culture is that people who might engage with your group or local church may have some of the same kinds of experiences that you were imagining in that foreign country a few moments ago. While your group or congregation may feel safe and familiar to *you*, it may feel quite different to newcomers seeking to engage with you. Some aspects of the beliefs that you share ('everyone knows that'), the things you do ('it's how we do it around here') and your language ('the way we say things') may be foreign to others. Imagine how someone in that foreign land you visited in your imagination might be able to help you to fit in, get involved and bring your own unique contribution. By being aware of the culture of your own group or congregation, you will be better able to ensure that people feel welcome, safe, valued and that they experience a sense of belonging.

There are many definitions of culture, but one of the most useful for our purposes is simply 'the way things get done around here'.[3] What follows is a series of activities to help you as you investigate 'the way things get done' in your group or congregation – and then as you examine what emerges in terms of how well it reflects or obscures the way of Christ and how well it ensures that those who don't currently belong within this group or congregation can do so with as few cultural barriers as possible. As the awareness of your group or congregational culture develops, may you be able to discern what should be celebrated and what must change – and may you have the courage and wisdom to embody and to implement any change that is necessary.

# Packing Our Bags:
# What to Take, what to Leave?

## Purpose

To enable groups or congregations to recognise those things which must be treasured, remembered and held onto – and other aspects of their shared life which can or should be left behind – as they embark or continue on their journey together.

The concept of 'journey' is an evocative metaphor for life in general and for the Christian life in particular. Within the scriptures, journeys provide a rich seam of instruction and wisdom. This simple activity is of particular value when a significant change is on the horizon, but can provide an effective exercise in refocusing at any time.

## Time required

60–90 minutes.

## Resources required

- Large sheets of paper, such as flip chart paper or lining paper.
- Plenty of marker pens – preferably of different colours.
- 1 table for every 6 people.
- Bell, hooter or similar.

# Instructions

1 Arrange the tables so that people can move easily from table to table. If there are participants with mobility difficulties, ensure that there is plenty of space for wheelchair access around the tables or that there are adequate chairs at each table, as appropriate. Otherwise this is an activity where people can stand around tables, although you will want a suitable area of seating for plenary feedback and discussion in the latter part of the session.

2 Place several marker pens (preferably of different colours) and a sheet of paper on each table. Each sheet of paper should have one of the following headings on it:
   • What we value about being part of (insert name of group or congregation).
   • What is distinctive about (insert name of group or congregation)?
   • Stories we tell about (insert name of group or congregation).

3 Divide the whole group into small groups of 5–7 people and instruct them to gather around one of the tables and spend 10–15 minutes sharing responses to the heading and writing these on the paper. Encourage people to chat as they engage in this exercise, but also emphasise that everyone should write down their responses and that something does not need to be discussed and agreed before being added.

4 After 10–15 minutes, sound a bell, hooter or similar, and instruct each group to move to a table with a different sheet on it and to discuss and note responses. Then repeat once more, so that everyone has responded to each of the three different headings.

5 Invite everyone to move around and review what has been written. Then ask them to place a tick next to each of only three statements which they think are particularly important.

6 Review the sheets in a plenary session, drawing particular attention to those statements which have been ticked. Ask the question, 'What have we learned about who we are?' and note responses on a flip chart.

7 Present three new sheets of paper, one headed 'We must remember / retain …'; one headed 'We could leave behind …'; and another headed 'Maybe …'. Invite people to suggest what might be written on each sheet – ensuring that things which emerge as controversial are listed under 'Maybe …' for further consideration.

# What next?

It can be useful to ask the question 'Why?' several times (as explained in 'Root Cause Analysis' on page 125) in order to identify the essence of what the group or congregation most value or, indeed, why those things they have identified as 'can be left behind' are no longer useful or relevant in the way that they perhaps were in the past.

# Song, Picture, Rescue: Discovering the Heart of Our Church Community

## Purpose

To help discover how we understand our church community's essential character.

Sometimes we can helpfully capture a moment or an idea not in a paragraph, but in an image or single word. This exercise is to help us do this for our church culture. It gives three variations on the basic theme of how an immediate, one-word response can clarify our understanding of our church community.

The first asks people to choose a song or a piece of music (it could be a general piece or a specifically Christian one), which, for them, would encapsulate their church culture. For example, what is their choice of Anthem for the church?

The second asks the group to think of the church community as a vehicle. Which one would they choose to represent the church?

The third asks them to imagine that the church property is on fire (or if there are no buildings, where all the church's belongings are stored). What one thing would they rescue?

## Time required

This depends on the number of people in the group. However, it should take no more than 30 minutes per question (this includes feedback and discussion). So, if the group is more than 8, divide them into smaller groups and give each small group 2–3 minutes to make their decision on one agreed choice.

## Resources required

- Flip chart.
- Marker pens.

## Instructions

> *'That was fun ... And interesting.'*

1 Decide if you are going to use one, two or all of the variations.
2 Explain to the group that you are going to ask them a question and that you want a quick reaction. Help them be comfortable with the idea that we know that this is not their thought-out, nuanced response.
3 Ask them to do this as individuals.
4 Ask the question. If you are using more than one variation, ask each question separately and after the responses have been given and discussed, move to the next variation.
5 When thinking about the song or piece of music, you could keep this completely open, or you could first limit it to a song or piece of music which was not created with the church in mind and then, if time, ask the question again using only the 'open' category.
6 Give people 1 minute maximum to think of their answer.
7 Ask people to share their choices and then, in 1 minute maximum, say why they made that choice.
8 Discuss the 'picture' built up from these choices. What does this say to the group as a whole?

## What next?

It might be helpful to repeat this exercise annually and note the changes, if any, that are made. What do these changes tell us?

## Ideas for visuals

If people are using the vehicle option, they might want to draw these. If so, pens and paper would need to be provided.

# Activities, Artefacts and Accounts: Taking a Fresh Look at Our Culture

## Purpose

To use 'activities' (i.e. what we do), 'artefacts' (i.e. physical facilities, décor, buildings) and 'accounts' (i.e. stories of the participants' experiences) as windows into the culture of our congregation or group. Then to use insights into our culture to see how our culture aligns with the Way of Jesus and a desire to be accessible and inclusive.

## Time required

90 minutes to 2 hours or, potentially, much longer, depending on the size and complexity of the congregation or group and the depth of the analysis.

The three aspects of this activity can be carried out simultaneously by three groups, with the groups then coming together for the analysis at the end – or in a way that involves everyone in every aspect, as in the instructions below. Another option is to split the activity across three or four different times, focusing on one aspect in each of three sessions and then, in a further session, undertake the analysis.

## Resources required

- Notepads or clipboards and paper, and pens.
- Marker pens.
- A selection of random images on cards (see 'Inspiring Conversations' activity on page 3).
- 3 sheets of flip chart paper or lining paper with columns and headings pre-marked as below:

| Activities **or** Artefacts **or** Accounts | What does this 'say' to 'us'? | What does this 'say' about the Way of Christ / Christian faith? | What does this 'say' to those who know nothing about our group/congregation? | Is there anything we should learn and/or do? |
|---|---|---|---|---|
| | | | | |
| | | | | |
| | | | | |

# Instructions

1 Ask people to suggest ways of collecting evidence of what this congregation or group actually 'does'. They might include things such as newsletters, notice sheets, magazines and notice-boards. Perhaps there are certain people who will be able to inform the group about particular areas of activity. Split participants into small groups and ask them to identify as many examples as they can of the activities associated with their group or church and note them in a notebook or on paper on a clipboard. If people are leaving the room to look at notice-boards or other sources, it is especially important to agree a clear time frame.

2 Explain that much of what we understand about ancient history is the result of archaeologists finding artefacts and interpreting them. These might include art, buildings, objects, etc. Our group or congregation will have a wide variety of artefacts associated with it, some symbolic, some very practical, but each telling us something about 'how we do things around here'. Send people in small groups to discover and list as many artefacts as possible.

3 Lay the picture cards out on tables, one set for each small group, and invite people to look at the pictures with this question in mind: 'Is there a picture here that says something to you about your experience of being part of this group or congregation?' Instruct them to do this in silence and not to pick any cards up, as others may also be looking at the same one. After a few minutes, ask people to share within their groups which card they chose and why. While they are speaking, others should listen intently and ask themselves the question: 'What does this "account" tell me about this congregation or group?' Encourage people to try and express this in just a word or two and to note it for each person they listen to.

4 Gather everyone together in a plenary session with the 'activities' analysis sheets (see above) in clear view. Instruct everyone to share 'activities' one by one until all have been noted. Then invite people to share insights related to each 'activity' in the next three columns. Follow the same process with the analysis sheets for 'artefacts' and 'accounts'.

5  Invite people to share suggestions regarding what has been learned and any action that should follow and note these in the final columns of the three analysis sheets.

## What next?

Collate proposed actions using the 'Traffic Lights' framework (things to stop, things to discuss, consider or change, things to start) in the 'Where Do We Start?' activity on page 138. Then use the 'Clustering' exercise in the 'Dreaming Dreams' activity on page 133 to discern whether there is consensus around certain suggestions and to prioritise options.

# Mixed Messages:
# What are We Saying about God?

## Purpose

To explore how different aspects of our corporate life in church reveal different understandings of God, by considering how our buildings, favourite hymns, style of worship, and so on can all express different things about God.

Sometimes these different understandings are complementary and lead to a more complete understanding of God, but they may also appear to be contradictory and confusing, sending mixed messages to people.

This exercise highlights the fact that not everyone sees or understands God in the same way, and this has a bearing on how people live and serve as disciples. There is nothing wrong with this; throughout Scripture different aspects of God's character are revealed to different people at different times.

## Time required

About 1 hour.

## Resources required

- Discussion cards (see sample at the end of the exercise).
- Paper and pens for making notes.
- Copies of a recent order of service.
- Copies of a recent church bulletin or magazine, or access to the church website.
- Flip chart paper and easel.
- Marker pens.

Check in advance what areas of the church buildings it will be possible to access at the time of the exercise.

# Instructions

1 Photocopy the sheet of discussion cards (below), and cut them into individual cards. There should be enough for each group to have one.

2 Arrange participants into groups, and explain the purpose of the exercise.

3 Give each group a card. More than one group can discuss the same topic. Ask someone in each group to read the card to the group. Allow a few minutes for this, and check that everyone is clear on their group's task.

4 Allow 30 minutes for the group to discuss their card. The group looking at buildings may want to walk around, or view the buildings from outside. The group discussing worship will need the orders of service. The group looking at activities will need copies of the church bulletin, or access to the church's website.

5 Bring the groups back together, and ask them to give feedback. On a flip chart sheet record their answers to their first question – what their area of discussion revealed about God. When each group has given their feedback, allow time for discussion. Is there a single cohesive picture of God emerging, or do different areas of the life of the church reveal different things? Are there any contradictions?

6 Repeat step 5 for the other two questions: What do their topics of discussion reveal about the church? What questions does this raise? Record the main points on a flip chart sheet.

7 Looking at the list of questions that the exercise has raised, ask participants to share in their groups if there are any that they would like to explore further. This is a personal response and the group needn't come to a consensus.

8 Finish the exercise in prayer, responding to how God has been revealed in the buildings, worship, welcome and activities of the church.

# Worksheet: Mixed Messages

Copy this and cut into separate cards for each group.

## Buildings

Take some time to think about the church's buildings, both the sanctuary and any other rooms or buildings.

Consider things like access, furnishings, art and signage as well as décor or state of repair.

If possible, take some time to walk round, and think about the following questions:

- If this building was all the information I had about God, what would it tell me?
- If this building was all the information I had about the church, what would it tell me?
- What questions might I want to ask?

## Worship

Take some time to think about the main worship service in the church. It may be helpful to have some sample orders of service to hand.

Consider things like the music style, who is involved in worship, the language used, the place of the sacraments, the sermon.

Think about the following questions:

- If the only information I had about God was from this church service, what would I understand?
- If the only information I had about the church was from this service, what impression would I get?
- What questions might it raise or answer?

## Welcome

Think about how we welcome people. Don't just think about the main worship service or the 'official' welcome – what about notice-boards, website, hospitality or mid-week activities?

It may help to consider how we would feel if we received the same sort of welcome in a non-church setting such as someone's home, a hotel or a coffee shop.

Think about the following questions:

- If the only information I had about God was in how I was welcomed, what would that tell me?
- If the only information I had about the church was in the welcome, what impression would I get?
- What questions might it raise?

## Activities

Make a list of the different groups and activities in the church. It may help to have a copy of the church bulletin or news sheet. Who are they for?

Remembering that the church is the Body of Christ, think about the following questions:

- If the activities of this church were all the information I had about God, what would I understand?
- If the activities of this church were all the information I had about the church, what would that tell me?
- What questions might they raise or answer?

# Strengths and Weaknesses: Checking Our 'Health'

## Purpose

To review five key areas of a congregation's ministry and to recognise those that are strongest and weakest. Thereafter, explore ways of building on the strengths and of addressing the weaknesses.

While it is possible to use this exercise with other groups, the aspects of health here apply to the breadth of purposes and activities of a church community. For groups with a particular focus, such as mission, friendship, social action and such like, facilitators should check that the different criteria can be fairly applied to the group in question.

## Time required

90 minutes–2 hours (a tea/coffee break is recommended, which would normally mean a session of two hours).

## Resources required

- Facilitator to lead the exercise (preferably not from the church community concerned).
- Flip chart easel and paper.
- Marker pens.
- Health Check Guide sheets (see first worksheet).
- Score sheets (see second worksheet).
- Spare pens.

# Instructions

## Preparation

Firstly, photocopy the required number of copies of the worksheets. You will need to have an idea of the numbers of people beforehand so that you can do this. It is wise to photocopy a few more than the number expected, just in case. The score sheets are for each individual person, so in this case, you will certainly need a good supply. The guide sheets are for each small group (seated around tables) to look at together, so you will need at least three or four sheets per group, depending on the size of the group.

On flip chart paper, draw a large, bold grid for scoring. In effect, it will be a large-scale version of the score sheet, but adding a total column (see second worksheet). This will help with 'tallying' the scores as an assisting person reads the individual score sheets out to you.

## Carrying out the exercise

1  Arrange everyone into small groups and ensure an appropriate number of guide sheets are on each table. Also ensure that every individual has a score sheet and a pen.

2  Explain the process: that each 'characteristic' will be explained, discussed and scored before moving on to the next. This way, everyone remains up to speed.

3  Read out the first characteristic and allow each group 2–3 minutes to discuss how weak/strong their church community is. They are not to agree on a score! It is merely an opportunity to gain more clarity before each person discreetly awards his or her own personal score. It must be stressed that the score is to be an honest reflection on the *congregation*, not on their own personal ability, faith journey and so on.

4  After a total of no more than 5 minutes for reading out, discussing and scoring, ensure everyone has placed *one* tick in the box of their choice along the first row of their score sheet. Once you are satisfied that everyone has placed their first tick, you may read out the second characteristic.

5  Repeat the process for each of the four remaining characteristics. Once everyone has placed their final tick, collect the sheets and call for the tea/coffee break.

6  Retire to a quiet corner of the room and with an assistant reading out the responses from the score sheets, tally the scores on the flip chart. Note that it is advisable to angle the flip chart easel away from general view until the time to reveal the final score totals. Use a bold marker pen, so that details will be clearly visible when you divulge the scores.

7  Each score given for 'very weak' is to be scored zero, for 'weak', one, 'strong', two and for 'very strong', three. (Therefore, as an example, seven ticks in the 'strong' category would score fourteen points and two in the 'very strong' category would score six.)

8  It is hoped that the totals can be added up in time for the completion of the tea break (10–15 minutes). Once everyone has returned to their seats, you can turn around the flip chart easel to reveal the scores and the totals for each characteristic. You can also

reveal the tally patterns, which may show common opinions or even very broad ranges of opinion.

9  It is hoped that a clear 'league table' will emerge, based on the totals for each characteristic. If any totals are the same, give the higher ranking to the characteristic that has scored more marks in the 'strong' and 'very strong' categories combined. If this is also the same (albeit unlikely), then simply separate them by alphabetical order.

10  Give each group a clean sheet of flip chart paper and invite a person in each group to be a scribe. Using 'portrait' mode, invite the scribes to divide the paper in two by drawing a straight line across the middle of the sheet.

11  Invite the scribes to write the strongest scoring characteristic at the top of the paper and to write the weakest scoring characteristic just under the dividing line. Then invite the groups to agree upon three short-term measures ('quick wins') that may help to build upon the strength and to list these in the top half of the sheet. Likewise, invite the groups to agree and list three short-term measures in the bottom half of the sheet that may help address the weakness. Allow 15–20 minutes for this exercise.

12  Conduct a plenary session in which each group is invited to report back on their six measures. Not all groups may have listed a full set of six measures, but encourage them to provide at least two for each characteristic during the task and to avoid dwelling for too long on either one.

# What next?

A follow-on exercise that looks at all five characteristics, but from an external perspective, will help provide a more rounded picture of the church community's health. This involves imagining a newcomer arriving and asking two questions for each of them: 'How might this characteristic help the newcomer in engaging with the life of the church community?' and 'How might this characteristic hinder the newcomer in engaging with the life of the church community?'

# Worksheets

There are two main documents to be photocopied. The first is in A4 format, while the second, once photocopied, will need guillotining in half to make A5 copies. As attendances can sometimes be unpredictable, always make sure to photocopy a reasonable number of spare copies in either case.

# Health Check

Please score (individually) on how 'healthy' you think your church community is in five main areas of ministry, based on Jesus' great commandments of loving God and our neighbours, along with his Great Commission of going out to 'make disciples'.

Your facilitator will guide you through the scoring process, but as an aid to your thinking, a brief description follows of these five equally important areas (listed alphabetically).

## Discipleship   Far more than listening to sermons

Church communities that are strong in this area are characterised by:

- Encouragement of personal spiritual disciplines (e.g. prayer and Bible reading).
- Nurture and encouragement of growth in character and faith through congregational activities and structures such as home groups or prayer groups.
- Young people and children not only learning Bible stories, but also learning how to apply Biblical themes into their daily lives.
- Fellowship that goes beyond that of mere socialising and involves such things as discussing faith issues, praying together and mentoring.

## Faith sharing   Far more than inviting someone to a coffee morning

Church communities that are strong in this area are characterised by:

- A clear understanding of the importance of sharing faith with others (faith should not be merely 'private' or 'personal').
- Enabling and encouragement of everyone to share their faith with family members, friends, work colleagues, etc.
- Possessing a culture of invitation, where members of the congregation invite family, friends and colleagues to services and other church-run events.
- Encouraging of those within the congregation who may be gifted as evangelists.

## Love and care   Far more than a cuppa after the church service

Church communities that are strong in this area are characterised by:

- Welcoming everyone with open doors and open arms, just as they are.
- Reaching out to the local community, seeking out where there are needs and taking practical steps to meet those needs.
- Having loving and caring relationships both within the church and in the wider community.

## Service   Far more than stacking some chairs

Church communities that are strong in this area are characterised by:

- Encouragement of loving service.
- Members partaking in the body of Christ by sharing their gifts, skills and resources.
- Members serving and engaging with the local community and environment.
- Being involved with issues of social justice, near and far, and supporting world mission.

## Worship   Far more than singing hymns on Sunday morning

Church communities that are strong in this area are characterised by:

- Having acts of shared worship that inspire people to offer themselves afresh to God.
- Providing opportunities for all present to understand and participate.
- Having variety, allowing people of differing temperaments to express their worship.
- Being concerned with the whole of life – not just church on a Sunday. This involves being concerned for each other's welfare, work and leisure and understanding there is no part of life where God is irrelevant.

# Health Check Score Sheet

(Please tick the box that **best describes** what you see happening in your church)

| Characteristic | Very Weak | Weak | Strong | Very Strong |
|---|---|---|---|---|
| Discipleship | | | | |
| Faith sharing | | | | |
| Love & care | | | | |
| Service | | | | |
| Worship | | | | |

# Health Check Score Sheet

(Please tick the box that **best describes** what you see happening in your church)

| Characteristic | Very Weak | Weak | Strong | Very Strong |
|---|---|---|---|---|
| Discipleship | | | | |
| Faith sharing | | | | |
| Love & care | | | | |
| Service | | | | |
| Worship | | | | |

# Invitation:
# Can We Become both
# Welcoming and Invitational?

## Purpose

To uncover the reasons why we don't invite people to church, and then look at what we could do in order to overcome those reasons.

When we think of what it means to receive an invitation to something, we usually think of a wedding or birthday party, an event to remember and look forward to in the weeks building up to the date. However, when it comes to inviting people to church, we do one of two things: either we make excuses for why they won't come, or we make excuses for why we shouldn't invite them. Both are based on assumptions which, at the core of them, are based on fear. A recent survey suggests that some 70% of Christians have someone in mind who they could invite to church, however, 80–95% of those have no intention of inviting anyone. In another survey, 1 in 5 people who weren't part of church said they would be open to attending and seeing for themselves what church, and God, is all about.

## Time required

1 hour.

## Resources required

- Flip chart easel and paper.
- Marker pens.
- 1 pen for each person.
- 1 Prayer List card (see below) for each person.

# Instructions

1 In groups of around 6, discuss what could be the reasons behind why we don't invite others to church, and record thoughts and views on a piece of flip chart paper.

2 Allow around 10 minutes for groups to complete the first task, followed by a time of feedback from each group, with the facilitator recording common opinions.

3 Ask the groups what could be done to overcome these fears, and record their thoughts, again allowing 10 minutes for discussion followed by a time of plenary feedback.

4 Hand out a 'prayer list' card to each person, asking them to spend time thinking and praying about who their five people could be, explaining the above statistic which shows that 1 in 5 people outside of the church would be open to an invitation to attend church.

5 Spend 5 minutes quietly filling the cards out, followed by a time of sharing with the person next to them.

6 Encourage people to spend time over the next few weeks praying for an opportunity to invite these people to church.


# What next?

Churches may benefit from working through our *Sharing Faith* resource, which can be found here – www.resourcingmission.org.uk/shop/sharing-faith. They also may wish to consider hosting a Weekend of Invitation event, where the church hosts an event to which congregation members can invite their friends or family. More information on this can be found here – www.resourcingmission.org.uk/mission/weekend-invitation

# Worksheet

So that people can take their prayer lists home to use, the blank lists could be photocopied directly onto small cards (rather than paper), or onto large self-adhesive address labels that are then fixed to postcards.

**Prayer List**

1_____

2_____

3_____

4_____

5_____

**Prayer List**

1_____

2_____

3_____

4_____

5_____

**Prayer List**

1_____

2_____

3_____

4_____

5_____

**Prayer List**

1_____

2_____

3_____

4_____

5_____

**Prayer List**

1_____

2_____

3_____

4_____

5_____

**Prayer List**

1_____

2_____

3_____

4_____

5_____

**Prayer List**

1_____

2_____

3_____

4_____

5_____

**Prayer List**

1_____

2_____

3_____

4_____

5_____

# The Secret Shopper:
# Rating Our Level of Welcome

## Purpose

To test out the congregation, organisation or group's welcome of newcomers or visitors and to seek improvements upon the findings.

While this exercise is written with church worship services in mind, it can be readily adapted to be used with other groups or activities.

## Time required

The duration of the church services to be reviewed will determine the timescale, but in addition, you will need about 2 hours for writing up a report.

## Resources required

You will need a small number of people (preferably not from the relevant group, although this is not vital) to take on certain roles.

## Instructions

The task can be carried out by members of the group, but to get a much more 'honest' response, it is advised that people unknown to them be involved. Understandably, their members will be more likely to behave in their usual way if they are unaware of the nature of the visit.

A 'group' of two adults and at least one young person should provide a suitable range of reaction and opinion.

The secret shoppers should begin by seeking out information on service, event or activity times. This involves ascertaining if there is a website and if so, what details are given. Furthermore, they are to look at the notice-board for information and even check local newspapers. They then judge how appealing the website and/or notice-board are to look at and note times for the visit.

## The visit

It is important to assume roles for the visit. Maybe one adult could pretend to be an agnostic and is contemplating the exploring of faith. Another could pretend to be a new Christian who is keen to make friends and enjoy some encouraging fellowship. The young person could simply be him or herself and assess the attitudes towards someone of his/her generation.

Upon entering the grounds, the team look around and check for tidiness and presentation. Is there any litter for example? Does the entrance area look inviting?

When entering the building, they should gauge the welcome that is offered. Each secret shopper should ask themselves these questions:

- Am I made to feel really welcome? (a friendly greeting, hearty handshake, etc.)
- Am I (and my colleagues) the centre of attention to those who greet me?
- Is anyone introducing themselves to me, or at least asking if I am new?
- Is the welcome area or the sanctuary providing any information on church activities?
- If so, is there any activity that is relevant to my assumed role?

For church worship services, when in the sanctuary, the secret shoppers may be familiar with the service style or with the type of décor, but they should try to see things as if they are completely new to them. Each should ask themselves these questions:

- While sitting in my pew or chair, is anyone greeting me?
- During the service, is there information relating to protocol (for example, standing for the Bible while it is brought in, giving verbal responses)
- Does anyone greet me or talk to me at the end of the service?
- Following the service, is there a time for refreshments?
- If there are refreshments, does anyone invite and accompany me to where they are?
- Does anyone come over to greet me during the time for refreshments?
- Are there signs directing me to where the toilets are?

## *After the visit*

Write up a report of the visit, each person giving their opinions in relation to their role. It would be wise to use constructive comments, beginning with the positives and to phrase the negative elements by way of suggested improvements or changes that may be made. The whole point of the exercise is to help congregations or groups put themselves into the shoes of a visitor and so honest responses (that may even be highly critical), need to be documented.

It is hoped that all the comments would be appreciated and that congregations or groups may look to build on any strengths, but also seek to address any weaknesses.

# Welcome, Hospitality and Belonging: From Guest to One of the Family

## Purpose

To identify what welcome and hospitality feel like. To explore the role of welcome and hospitality in engendering a sense of belonging. To identify practical steps to creating a greater sense of welcome and belonging.

This exercise uses an appreciative enquiry approach. There may well be things which have caused people to feel distinctly unwelcome, but focusing on this could result in a negative and demotivating session.

## Time required

About 1 hour.

## Resources required

- 4 large sheets of paper per group – flip chart paper is ideal.
- Marker pens.
- Sticky notes.

# Instructions

1 Arrange participants in small groups around tables, equipped with paper, marker pens and sticky notes, and explain the purpose of the exercise.

2 As a connecting-up exercise, ask participants to turn to the person next to them, and share about a time when they felt really welcome. What factors contributed to this sense of welcome? Allow 5 minutes for this.

3 To the whole group, ask the following question, recording responses on a flip chart.
   • Who do we offer welcome and hospitality to?
   (Here we are looking for categories of people, e.g. visitors, friends or family. This is a general question, and not just applicable to church). This should only take a few minutes.

4 Working now in groups, ask each group to split one of the flip chart sheets into two columns headed 'Guest' and 'Family'. Invite the groups to discuss the difference between being a guest and being part of the family. They should record responses on the flip chart sheet. Some possible responses include:
   *Guests:* Come by arrangement, only stay for a while, don't own anything, aren't responsible for anything, receive hospitality and so on.
   *Family:* Come and go as they please, they live here, they have ownership and responsibility, offer hospitality to others.
   Allow 5–6 minutes for this.

5 Next, ask the groups 'How do we want people to feel when they come to church – like guests, part of the family, or something else, and why?' This can generate some discussion, so allow more time for this. It is likely that people will identify positive and negative aspects of each. Different people will also define 'church' differently – just the worship service, or perhaps any activity run by the church. This is fine. Allow 10–12 minutes for this, then take some feedback from the different groups.

6 The second half of the exercise concentrates on the specifics of this church. On sticky notes, ask people to write down what has made them feel welcome in this church community or group – writing one thing on each note. Ask them to stick them onto a flip chart sheet, and arrange them into clusters of similar comments. Allow the groups to discuss this, and encourage people to share their stories of when they felt welcome. Allow 6–7 minutes for this.

7 Following the same process as step 6, this time ask the group to identify what helped them move from feeling like a visitor, to feeling like part of the church. There is a chance that some people might not feel like that – in that case ask them what would give them a greater sense of belonging. This might be harder for people to identify than the previous question, so allow a little more time for this – around 10 minutes.

8 Take some feedback from the whole group, asking what the main clusters of comments were at their table. This provides a list of what the church is now doing, with some success, in hospitality and welcome.

9  Looking at the list, ask each group to discuss one way in which they can help people know they are welcome, and one way they can help visitors feel like they really belong. Allow 10 minutes for this and take feedback, recording it on a flip chart.

10  To finish, ask what the next steps should be. This could be referring this list to the leadership group, or perhaps people making a personal commitment to making the church a more welcoming place. Close in prayer, including these next steps, and praying in thanks for visitors to the church.

# Comparing Priorities: Stated and Actual

## Purpose

To assess the degree to which the actions of a committee, group or team reflect stated priorities.

Whether you are a member of a church congregation or some other kind of group, the chances are that there is some kind of committee or team responsible for leadership and management. When this activity has been completed, it will be possible to identify steps to ensure that the work of the team or committee is well aligned with the reason for the congregation or group's reason for existence and the things that it deems most important.

## Time required

1–2 hours.

## Resources required

- Copies of the purpose statement or mission statement for the group or congregation – enough copies for 1 per small group.
- Copies of agendas for the last three meetings and/or a set of accounts for the past year and/or a budget for the current period – for each small group.
- Multi-coloured marker pens.
- A5 pieces of paper or card.
- Flip chart paper.

# Instructions

1 Invite people to form small groups and spend a few minutes re-familiarising themselves with the purpose statement or mission statement. Instruct each group to break down the statement into its constituent themes or topics and write these on some of the A5 cards – one theme or topic per card – and to spread these on the table or floor where they are clearly visible to them.

2 Ask the groups to review the agendas, accounts or budgets in the light of these themes or topics. The marker pens can be used to highlight on these documents those sections which relate to one of the elements of the purpose or mission statement. This can be done by allocating colours or symbols to the different themes. Depending on the complexity and size of these documents and the amount of time available, it may be preferable to assign different sets of papers to different groups: for example, one group look at agendas and others at budgets and/or accounts.

3 Explain that each group has now created a visual reflection of the way in which time and resources are allocated to the themes/topics which are stated as being fundamental to their reason for existence. Ask the groups to assess the attention given to each theme/topic, using the following scale: 1 = total neglect; 2 = minimal attention; 3 = some attention; 4 = considerable attention; 5 = highest attention. Write this scale on a flip chart so all can refer to it as necessary.

4 Gather in plenary session and ask each group to share their assessment, using a flip chart to collate their findings: Which areas appear to be given the highest priority? Is this appropriate? Which areas are neglected? Does the mission/purpose statement need amending or does the allocation of time, attention and resources need to be addressed? Are there some themes/topics which have been assessed differently by different groups? If so, why might this be so?

5 Conclude with plenary collection of ideas and responses under three headings: What have we learned? What do we feel challenged about? What actions are we going to take?

## What next?

To discern whether there is consensus around the actions suggested, use the 'Clustering' exercise in the 'Dreaming Dreams' activity on page 133 or the 'Voting' exercise in 'Where Do We Start?' on page 138.

This activity works especially well with a well-defined group such as a committee or small team. However, by looking at how a whole congregation or organisation uses its time and resources, it is possible to use the same techniques to assess its alignment to, or departure from, its stated purpose or mission.

# Section 4
# UNDERSTANDING OUR COMMUNITIES

# Introduction

'Who is my neighbour?' a religious scholar asked Jesus. When we read about this encounter in Luke's Gospel, we discover that the question was not entirely sincere. The enquirer was trying to 'test' Jesus; he wanted to 'justify himself' or, as one contemporary translation puts it, 'Looking for a loophole, he asked, "And just how would you define 'neighbour'?"' (Luke 10:29). As was his habit, not only did Jesus sidestep a simplistic definition, he went on to tell a story and, in so doing, turned the question on its head. In hearing the profound and shocking parable of the Good Samaritan, the expert in religious law was challenged to go and demonstrate love and mercy. Likewise, as we consider our own community – the needs of neighbours, the opportunities for loving service and challenges that confront us – we too are provoked to reconsider how we respond.

Whether our church or group is in a small village or a huge city, we are called to understand and respond in love to our community. Often there are people within our congregations and groups who have a real passion for the community on the doorstep. They have a finger on the pulse of what is going on and want to see the Christian community being salt and light. There may well be others who are recent arrivals. They are just learning about the area, its people and what makes things tick here; while lacking detailed knowledge, they are able to see things through fresh eyes. The perspectives of each person will be unique and valuable. The exercises in this section will help bring together everyone's insights and experiences in order to gain a richer, fuller understanding of the community. They have the potential to open the eyes of participants to things they were previously unaware of, issues they had not considered and possibilities hitherto unconsidered.

For some congregations, 'parish' is an important reality. It defines a people and place they have a particular concern for. The word 'parish' comes from the Greek word *paroikos*, meaning 'the stranger who lives alongside'. Our mission always begins by being alongside people and the activities in the section will enable a better understanding of where people are and the different things which bring people together. Some 'parish churches' draw a substantial proportion of their congregation from beyond the parish boundaries. It is helpful to build up a picture of where the people God has brought together actually live, work and spend their time.

Some churches understand their call to be part of God's mission in terms that are not particularly geographical. The focus of their mission might be defined by demographic, linguistic or any number of characteristics. Increasingly people live life in networks of work and leisure which may or may not overlap with a local neighbourhood.

However community is expressed, here are some activities which, when undertaken with care, prayer and as wide a participation as possible, can deepen understanding, raise awareness and help to identify possible responses. Better understanding our context will raise questions of how we shape our church life to the context, or how we maintain our distinctiveness, or – in the face of injustice or oppression – how we become a community of resistance.

We read that, on becoming aware of the situation of his own people in Jerusalem, Nehemiah was moved to prayer. Stirred by what he heard, he could have been tempted to leap into action. However, we are told that 'he sat down' and he prayed (Neh. 1:4). Later, having arrived on site in Jerusalem, he took time to inspect the walls of the city, carefully assessing the situation. We do well to follow his example of beginning and continuing in prayer – and then investing time in seeking to understand the context well. Such an approach differentiates the discerning of God's mission from mere well-intentioned activity. In this section you will find tools that enable people to gain fresh insights into their community and, having done so, to consider how they respond. Responses might include prayers, loving service, encouraging or supporting what others are already doing, campaigning or challenging where injustice or particular needs are identified, etc.

# Who is My Neighbour?: Getting to Know the Community

## Purpose

To listen to, and understand better, the community that the church is part of; to enable the church to love and serve the community in relevant and meaningful ways; to identify ways that the church can respond to needs in the area.

This exercise may be used in conjunction with one of the mapping exercises in this book, or the 'Do We Know Our Community?' quiz on p. 94.

## Time required

About 1 hour.

## Resources required

- A map, or statistical information about the community, to help participants visualise the people who live in the area. If the group has already done one of the mapping exercises or the 'Do We Know Our Community?' quiz on p. 94, then the information collected in those exercises may be used.
- 2 sheets of A4 paper per group.
- 1 pen for each participant.
- 1 large sheet of paper (flip chart or lining paper is ideal) for each group.
- At least 1 flip chart or marker pen per group.

# Facilitator notes

We often bring assumptions to what we do. One common assumption is that the way we do things is the way everyone else does it too, and it can be easy to think of our churches as being a useful microcosm of the wider community. It is helpful to examine this assumption – and to do it more than once. Communities change and develop, and even if we were once intimately acquainted with the people and cultures, there will always be new information to unearth and fresh discoveries to be made.

This exercise is a good way of collecting a lot of perceptions about the community from the congregation. It is important to note, that while this is useful, it will not provide an in-depth or empirical analysis of the community. In most cases, congregations or other church groups are not representative of the wider population, so the findings from this exercise can't be extrapolated to represent the views or opinions of the wider community. This exercise is most useful as a step to identifying what further engagement with the community would be useful. It is most beneficial to have a balance of facts and figures – statistical information, surveys, and such like, with qualitative information. There is no substitute for actually meeting people and talking with them. The What next? section is therefore important to consider how to get maximum benefit from this.

# Instructions

1 Arrange participants into groups around tables.
2 Ask each group to write the heading 'Our Neighbours' on one sheet of A4 paper, and then to list the different groups or types of people who live or gather in the area around the church. For example, are there any nursing homes, people who don't speak English as a first language, shift workers? Is the community ageing, or are there large numbers of families? Are there schools or shopping centres? Is the population seasonal: for example, students or people working through holiday seasons? Allow around 10 minutes for this.
3 Invite the groups to share what they have written with the larger group. If there are a large number of groups it may be helpful to limit each group to two or three answers. Allow a few minutes for people to respond to this, sharing particularly what they found surprising or unexpected.
4 Working again in small groups, invite participants to put the heading 'Good News' on the second sheet of A4 paper and consider just one of the groups of people they identified in step 2. Ask, 'What would be good news for these people?' and invite the groups to list as many possible answers as they can. At this stage, avoid focusing specifically on the church's response to the needs identified; the idea is to have a general picture of what different people would welcome: for example, the hungry might welcome food, the lonely might welcome company. The point here is to increase the creative potential of the group. Allow about 15 minutes for this.

5 The groups will now have the opportunity to consider how their own congregation might become 'good news' to its neighbours. Using the large sheets of paper, invite each group to head the paper with the people they had considered in step 4. Ask them to draw three concentric circles on the paper, like a target, as large as the paper will allow. The centre circle is 'Things within our control'. The second circle is 'Things we can influence but not control'. The outer circle is 'Things beyond our influence'.

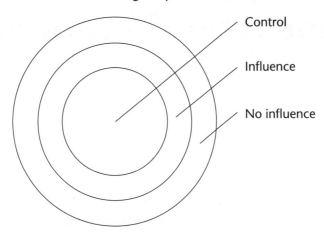

6 Invite the groups to look at the list they made in step 4. Consider whether each item is something that would be within the church's power or authority to do, and write these in the centre circle. If the item is something that the church could support or influence, but only do with the partnership, support or permission of others, add this to the centre circle. Things that are currently beyond the church's ability to influence should go in the outer circle. Allow around 20 minutes for this.

7 As each group finishes, stick their completed sheet to a wall, or lay out on a table. Encourage participants to take time to look at the responses from other groups.

8 Invite feedback in the larger group. Are there any common themes which have emerged? What has struck people? What has prompted further questions? Finish with prayer, inviting people to pray in their groups for their neighbours, and particularly for the group of people they have been discussing.

## What next?

The leadership of the church may want to consider this further. Some questions which may help are:

- Who else do we need to share this with?
- What people or issues in our community have been overlooked?
- What further information do we need?
- Who do we need to talk to in the community?
- What is the 'good news' that we are able to share with our neighbours?
- Who can we work alongside in the community?

# Influence Mapping:
# What Shapes this Community?

## Purpose

To develop a better understanding of what shapes the local community.

Small groups use their knowledge, insights and wisdom to create a visual representation of what makes the community what it is. This develops awareness of opportunities and challenges for their congregation or group.

## Time required

40 minutes–1 hour.

## Resources required

For each small group:

- 1 large (e.g. A2 / flip chart) sheet of paper – pre-marked with a series of 4–6 concentric rings (i.e. like a target) filling the whole page.
- Sticky notes (10–15 per person).
- 1 pen per person.
- 1 A4 sheet of paper headed 'OPPORTUNITIES'.
- 1 A4 sheet of paper headed 'CHALLENGES'.

# Instructions

1 Arrange people into small groups and explain the purpose of the activity.

2 Encourage everyone to contribute by naming influences, writing these on sticky notes and placing them on the map. They should place powerful influences near the centre; weaker influences closer to the edge.

3 Encourage people to discuss their perspectives throughout. The facilitator may want to ask some questions to stimulate further contributions when the discussion begins to slow. For example: What are the things that attract people to this community? Are there things that lead to people leaving? Where is the church in all of this – the different aspects of church life, different churches? What are the influences from outside the community that help to shape it – for better or worse? What brings people together here? What is here for particular age groups? What are the places and activities that members of the congregation or group are involved in?

4 Once there is a sense of contributions slowing down and groups have expressed their main ideas on the maps, invite groups to look at each other's maps, then to return to their own and make any additions in the light of what they have seen.

5 Invite people to sit quietly, reflect on the map they have created and ask themselves the questions: What opportunities do you see here for this congregation or group? What challenges for this congregation or group are highlighted by this understanding of the community? After a while invite people to share their thoughts within their group and note ideas on the sheets provided.

'The mapping exercise brought together the perspectives of people who live in different parts of the parish and people of different ages ... As we looked at the "map" we'd made, we could see that some of the difficult challenges for people in our community are also opportunities for the church.'

'It was a real eye-opener to realise all the different things folk are involved in. Yes, "the church" is not the most powerful influence in the community, but it's amazing how many of us are involved in the things we felt were the most influential things.'

## What next?

Groups could feedback their insights in a plenary session and ask the question: how should we respond to these opportunities and challenges? Activities from the *Discerning Our Future* section of this resource could be used to enable people to prioritise ideas and identify first steps.

# Cuttings:
# Collage Mapping

## Purpose

To give an opportunity to express our understanding of our community using everyday images.

Not everyone finds words the easiest way to express what they think, believe or feel. This activity uses images from newspapers and magazines to form a collage and through this, enable individuals and groups to express their understanding of the communities and cultures which the church serves and aspires to serve. This activity could also be used to help people express their understanding of the church community.

For those who are comfortable with words, but perhaps not with images, it allows them:

- to look at something in a fresh way;
- to recognise how those who are not as verbally articulate may, at times, feel.

## Time required

About 1 hour, although this may vary, depending on the size of group and if people are working individually, in pairs or groups.

## Resources required

- A large and varied stock of newspapers and magazines. Try to ensure that local papers/freebies/flyers are included.
- Large sheets of blank paper.
- Scissors.
- Glue.
- Felt-tip pens.

# Instructions

1 Explain to people that they are going to describe the communities and cultures which the church serves and aspires to serve and that they are going to do this by creating a collage using pictures or headlines from magazines and newspapers.
2 Decide together if this will be done individually, in pairs or in small groups (some people may have difficulty using scissors, or feel at a creative loss).
3 Give people 20 minutes to create their collage.
4 Give each person/pair/small group 1–2 minutes to describe their collage.
5 Discuss with the whole group what general 'picture' emerges when they put together the ideas behind the collages.

> 'This approach helps us look at our community with fresh eyes.'

# What next?

Discuss how this impression relates to information which has been gathered about the community from other sources such as government statistics, other forms of mapping or prayer walking.

# Ideas for visuals

Visuals are intrinsic to the activity.

# One Thing I ...:
# Assets and Change

## Purpose

To help us focus on the positive features of our community: the assets, while being honest about what we would like to change to make a positive difference.

## Time required

About 60–90 minutes, depending on the size of the group.

## Resources required

- Flip chart.
- Felt-tip pens.

## Instructions

> 'This is something that
> all ages can do.'

1 Explain to people that they are going to be thinking about the communities and cultures, which the church serves and aspires to serve. Be clear about which community or culture is being considered, e.g. geographical, demographic, interest.
2 Ask them, as individuals, to think of one thing that they like or admire about the community or culture being considered, e.g. if a visitor were to ask them what is great about this community, how would they respond? Give them one minute to do this.
3 Give everyone one minute each to share their thoughts.
4 Discuss what picture of the community this gives.

5  Now ask everybody to think of one thing that they would like to change within the community or culture being considered.
6  Again, give everyone one minute each to share their thoughts.
7  Discuss the picture of the community that this gives.
8  Discuss the picture that builds up when you put together the responses to both questions.
   - Is this what people expected?
   - Does this provide a helpful insight into the community?
   - Does it give a 'true' picture of the community?
   - In what ways is the Kingdom of God reflected in this composite picture/snapshot and in what ways does the life of the Kingdom challenge the community?

## What next?

1  How might this composite picture/snapshot help the group love and serve the community and help them identify a potential basis for partnerships within it?
2  Think about opportunities, how and where, you could involve the community in this activity. For example: sponsor a school art/photography project to depict children's answers to these two questions and then hold a community display of the children's work. This could also be done with adult groups that meet within the community.

## Ideas for visuals

Some people may give their response as an image, be prepared to draw (even badly) or have someone lined up to do this.

# Do We Know Our Community? Let's have a Quiz!

## Purpose

To help understand the demographics of the local community, as recorded from current census data and, where appropriate, to highlight any pertinent statistics of interest.

## Time required

30 minutes (plus time for feedback).

## Resources required

- Statistical information (see instructions below).
- 1 quiz sheet per group.
- 1 pen per group.
- A suitable prize (e.g. a box of chocolates).
- An answer sheet (to read out at the end of the quiz – obviously).

## Instructions

### Preparation beforehand

1  Both the Church of Scotland and the Church of England provide parish statistics from the latest census data. These can be found at www.churchofscotland.org.uk (on the home page, look for section named, 'Your local church' and follow prompts) and at https://www.churchofengland.org/about-us/facts-stats/research-statistics.aspx (click on map,

type in name of place, click on green dot that represents your church, see tab that appears and go to '2 of 2')

2 From available statistics, choose those of particular pertinence or interest and prepare multiple-choice answers to between 10 and 20 questions, depending on the time available for the quiz. Write out the question sheets with the choice of answers, A, B, C or D and photocopy the required number (one per team). Also photocopy an answer sheet to read out after the allotted time for questions.

3 Ensure each 'team' around the tables has a quiz question sheet and a pen.

4 Prepare a tie-break question in case there is a tie for the top score.

## Carrying out the exercise

1 Read out the questions, allowing for conferring and deliberation from all the teams. Even though each team will have the questions in front of them, it is advisable to read them out, so that you can keep everybody 'up to speed' and to enable you run the quiz at the pace of your choosing, so as to keep punctual.

2 Allow a few moments after reading out the last question for teams to check through their papers and that they have answered all the questions.

3 It would be disappointing if it was necessary to swap answer sheets for marking, so allow each team to mark their own papers honestly, as you read out the answers. After requesting each team's score (asking a tie break question if necessary), award the winning team a small prize. Just for fun, you might choose to award the lowest scoring team a 'booby prize' of a cheap, wooden spoon!

## Feedback

It is likely that all teams will not score very highly and there will have been answers that have surprised a number of people. Therefore a short plenary session to discover what people learned from the quiz would be helpful. Suggested questions could include:

• What facts surprised or shocked you?
• In what way(s) did some of the statistical data change your perceptions of the community?
• Did the statistics indicate any areas or groups within the community that the church is not engaging with?
• What opportunities for outreach do the statistics provide?

It is possible (although rare) that some people may feel embarrassed at low scores, so if you are aware of this, make sure you include one or two much easier questions and upon announcing the scores, reassure everyone that low scoring is quite normal.

## What next?

In the light of the feedback, a small working group may be set up to investigate matters further. There are usually a number of local community groups and support agencies that would be willing to engage in conversation with the local church, with a view to fostering partnerships. The statistics may indicate certain needs in the community that such partnerships may help to meet.

Despite recent drops in attendances across a vast number of congregations, such statistics often indicate a profession of Christian faith on a greater scale. This may encourage initiatives that are centred on a culture of invitation.

# Parish Mapping: Visualising Our Community

## Purpose

Understanding our context and those within our community is vital when it comes to knowing how to engage with the community.

This exercise allows us to visualise the community within a defined geographical area, gaining insight into who the people are and where they live, as well as highlighting any opportunities for mission. The defined area may be parish boundaries, as referred to in the title, but may be defined by other boundaries, such as town or village, or within a particular radius or distance.

## Time required

30–40 minutes.

## Resources required

- Flip chart paper.
- Marker pens.

## Instructions

1 Within small groups, agree on the area boundaries, and begin to draw out your map, highlighting the following:
   - Any housing estates.
   - Other churches.
   - Shops/local amenities.

- Parks.
- Transport links.

2 Once you have completed this, spend some time as a group highlighting where each person lives. For those living outside the area, mark on the map the direction of where you live, for example, if you live to the north of the area, place a dot in that direction.

3 Spend some time within your groups discussing the following questions:
- Where are the people we have not reached?
- What could we do to reach out to them?
- Are there any possible partnership opportunities with other churches or organisations in the community?

## What next?

One outcome from this exercise is seeing where the people are who are yet to be reached, and so a possible next step would be to look at ways in which the church could reach out to them. Could the church organise a special event of some description to which they could be invited? Perhaps a flyer drop, giving information on the church and its programmes, could help to make an initial connection.

# Parish Timeline: Discovering Our Past to Shape Our Future

## Purpose

To remind the group of events that have taken place both within the church and its community which have had an impact on the life of the church over the years.

Ministers and leaders new to their post have greatly benefited from this exercise as a way of understanding the local context and how the church came to be.

## Time required

40 minutes–1 hour.

## Resources required

- Lining paper (approx. 4ft long).
- Masking tape to secure lining paper to the table.
- Marker pens (approx. 4 per group).
- Flip chart easel and paper to record findings at the end of the exercise.
- Laptop and projector, with slides explaining exercise.

## Instructions

1  Work in small groups, seated around tables with lining paper set up on each table.
2  Explain the exercise, giving the following instructions (it may be useful to prepare one in advance as a visual aid):

a Draw a horizontal line along the middle of the lining paper, and above the line write 'Celebrations', with 'Struggles' below.

b About 12 inches from the left-hand side of the paper, draw a vertical line from top to bottom. In this section, write 'Pre-1980'.

c Along the timeline, mark out 10-year increments, starting at 1980 right up to the present year.

d Allow around 30–40 minutes to complete the timeline, asking the groups to write down all celebrations and struggles both within the church and the community, dating back to 1980, with any major events prior to 1980 to be recorded in the sectioned off part on the left of the lining paper.

3 Allow time for people to walk around the room at the end, looking at the other groups' timelines, and noting any common themes or similarities. Record these on the flip chart for all to see.

## What next?

The information gathered from this exercise can help to shape future activities and outreach programmes, as the church learns from its past, and gains a greater understanding of the history of the community. It may also be worthwhile to work through further mapping exercises.

# Appreciative Mapping: Identifying Our Communities' Strengths and Weaknesses

## Purpose

To spend time looking at what is going on within the community, both positive and negative.

From this, there will be opportunity to discuss what could be done to build on the positive features of the parish, as well as looking at how to address what the group perceive to be the negative features.

## Time required

40 minutes–1 hour.

## Resources required

- 1 sheet of flip chart paper per group.
- 2 marker pens per group.
- Flip chart for feedback.

## Instructions

1 Set the room up with chairs around tables, no more than 6 chairs per table.
2 Explain the exercise to the groups, asking each to draw a line down the centre of their paper, and on one side draw a ☺ and the other a ☹.
3 Allow time for the groups to complete both lists (around 20 minutes).

4  Ask each group to highlight 2–3 comments from both the positive and negative sides and ask:
   • Does the church currently have involvement/influence in these areas?
   • If so, what?
   • If not, could the church do something?
   Ask the group to identify 2–3 practical things which could be put in place over the coming couple of months.
5  Have a time of feedback for the whole group, recording comments on a flip chart.

## What next?

The purpose of this exercise is to identify areas within the community where the church could have a positive impact and influence. The group may want to meet again in order to look at the practical ideas they have identified and to agree on how best to achieve these goals within a realistic period of time.

# Section 5

# LEARNING FROM OUR EXPERIENCES

# Introduction

I wonder what comes to mind when you hear the word 'learning'? For many people 'school' would be one of the first things – with positive or negative connotations, depending on our experiences of what are sometimes called the 'best years of your life'. However, although there can be a tendency to associate 'learning' with formal education or training, the fact is that, throughout the whole of our lives, we are learning everywhere and all the time. We learn values, attitudes, skills, virtues, beliefs and ideas. We learn from our own experiences and we learn by observing and listening to other people.

Learning is intrinsic to being human, but for those who have responded to the call of Jesus to 'follow me', it takes on particular meaning and importance. We are 'disciples', life-long learners who have embarked on the adventure of growing and being formed into ever greater Christlikeness. For some people, formal training has a valuable role in their Christian development. However, for most of us, learning to be followers of Christ is primarily an informal and hotchpotch affair. Whatever our particular preferences, opportunities and limitations, we are all on a journey of God-ward transformation. We are being changed. God has sent the 'Spirit of truth' to guide us 'into all the truth' (John 16:13).

Each disciple's walk with Christ is unique. We all have particular things to learn and to unlearn as, in his wisdom and love, he forms us in his own image. However, the road of discipleship is rarely, if ever, travelled alone. To be called to Christ is to be a member of a worldwide family, part of his body, the Church. When asked to teach his disciples how to pray, Jesus did not instruct them to pray 'My Father', but 'Our Father'. At the same time we become a follower of Jesus, we instantaneously become brother or sister to many millions across the globe and throughout eternity. It's quite a thought.

This family, in all its diverse expressions, as well as being a vital source of learning for the individual Christian, is also on a shared journey of transformation. Paul refers to the Church as the 'bride of Christ' and explains that Jesus 'gave up his life for her to make her holy and clean, washed by the cleansing of God's word. He did this to present her to himself as a glorious church without a spot or wrinkle or any other blemish' (Eph. 5:25–7, New Living Translation). Therefore, as well as the learning inherent in our personal Christian growth, there is also a kind of corporate learning, as *together* we grow into greater unity and holiness.

The Church is called to embody and demonstrate radical, self-giving, love – both among believers and towards all. The New Testament exhorts us to 'be devoted to one another' (Rom. 12:10), 'serve one another' (Gal. 5:13) and 'carry each other's burdens' (Gal. 6:2). Indeed we are instructed to 'one another' each other in nearly 60 different ways.

For most of us (well, *all* of us actually), attaining the benchmark the Bible sets for Christians, 'the whole measure of the fullness of Christ' (Eph. 4:13) is a tall order. It requires a lifetime of learning of the most profound and varied kind: new values, reformed behaviours, transformed priorities, a whole-of-life reorientation. The same applies to our corporate life together, whether as a local congregation or any Christian group or organisation.

We *will* learn. That is certain. Even without intentional effort on our part, the experiences of life and the work of God's Spirit will shape us and the communities of faith we are part of. However, to be faithful followers requires a conscious commitment to learning. The activities in this section are tools to enable *deliberate shared* learning. If we are devoted to developing congregations and groups that are life-giving and love-permeated, inviting and inclusive, encouraging and demanding, then we need to learn how to learn together. Here are some tried and tested tools to assist that exhilarating and exacting journey.

# Three Ways to See: Observing, Wondering, Realising

## Purpose

To use a framework based on the resurrection account in John's Gospel to reflect upon and learn from any kind of experience, positive or negative.

Reflecting in this way enables us to learn from our experiences and, if it becomes a regular practice in our group or congregation, will provide a highly effective means of continuous learning and refining. The use of 'Values Based Reflective Practice' (VBRP®) in many parts of the health and social services is based on this same framework, originally developed by Michael Paterson, chaplain at St Columba's Hospice in Edinburgh. For anyone wanting to explore VBRP® in greater depth, the *National Handbook for Best Practice* is freely available online.[4]

## Time required

45–90 minutes.

## Resources required

Flip chart and marker pens.

## Instructions

1  Explain that the original Greek text of John's account of the resurrection includes three different words which we often translate as 'see' or 'saw'. By digging into their different

meanings we discover a helpful framework for reflection on any incident or experience with a view to gaining better understanding.

2 Invite people to listen out for the words 'see' or 'saw' and then read John 20:1–10.

3 Ask people when they spotted the first incidence of the word 'see' or 'saw'. (It first appears in relation to Mary when we are told in v. 1 that she 'went to the tomb and *saw* that the stone was moved away from the entrance'.) Explain that this example translates the Greek word *blepo*, which literally means 'she saw with her eyes' or 'she noticed'. Write on the flip chart: '1 To see, notice or observe'.

4 Ask the group when they spotted the second occurrence of the word 'see' or 'saw'. It is used again in many English translations in v. 5 where we are told that Simon Peter 'bent down to look in [the tomb] and *saw* the linen wrappings lying there' (NRSV). Explain that the word translated here is the Greek word *thereo* which means 'to see and to wonder' and that it is the word from which we get our English word 'theory'. In other words, Simon Peter not only noticed these cast aside objects, but he began to construct theories about what had happened, he wondered what it meant. Write on the flip chart: '2 To wonder or be curious'.

5 Ask participants when they spotted the third example of the word 'see' or 'saw'. (It occurs again in many English translations in v. 8 when we are told that 'the other disciple … *saw* and believed'.) Explain that the word translated here is the Greek word *choreo*, which means 'to realise', so, 'I see!', in the sense of 'the penny has dropped'. Write on the flip chart: '3 To realise'.

6 Explain that these three different words represent three different levels of seeing, a journey into greater understanding. First, to see with the eyes, then to wonder (to apply the mind to what is seen) and, finally, to realise (to come to some new understanding, to gain fresh insight, as a result of seeing and wondering).

7 Now apply this framework to the particular experience, incident or event by brain storming under each heading on the flip chart. Start by inviting people to share what happened, what was observed. Then invite people to 'be curious', to wonder, to raise questions and possible explanations, to 'theorise'. Finally, ask what we can realise. This may lead to discussing some actions that need to be taken; it may be appropriate just to note the learning and carry it into the future.

# The Heroic Journey:
# Growing through Challenges

## Purpose

To look at how our shared history experience enables us to reflect how we are maturing as a community of disciples (see James 1:2–4).

This exercise provides a framework to help us recognise the positive, formational role of challenges and crises in our Christian life, both individually, and as Christian communities.

## Time required

60–90 minutes.

## Resources required

- A flip chart – prepare one worksheet with the Timeline Cycle diagram shown below.
- Marker pens.

For each group:

- A long sheet of paper – frieze paper or lining paper is ideal for this.
- A large worksheet with the Timeline Cycle Diagram shown below – at least A3 size. A sheet of flip chart paper is ideal.
- A selection of marker pens.
- Sticky notes.

# Facilitator notes

Growth and development don't happen in our comfort zone. They occur when we are challenged, stretched, pushed to a place where our normal approach is no longer sufficient. Patience is only acquired by being in a situation that requires patience. Stamina is developed by doing things that require endurance. Compassion develops when we are faced with need. This is as true for communities and groups of people as it is for individuals.

In the first half of the twentieth century, mythologist Joseph Campbell identified a pattern, which he called the Monomyth, or hero journey, which was common to the stories of many cultures throughout the ages, including the narratives contained in the Christian Bible.[5] It showed that our response to challenge – to the call to move out of the familiar – has the potential to be transformative, and result in people and communities who are a great blessing in the world. It provides a helpful framework to help us to look back and to learn from our experience. The diagram below shows the elements of this framework, which we will be using in this exercise.

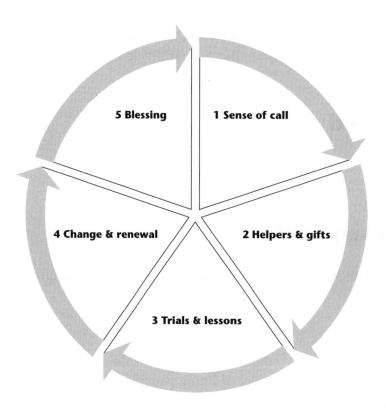

Unlike a linear timeline, this cycle does not necessarily follow a chronological order. We may go from section 2 to 3, then back again, before continuing.

1  **Sense of call.** The cycle begins with a sense that we have been called to something – a new challenge, a journey, a change of direction.
2  **Helpers and gifts.** On our discipleship journey we have been provided with gifts, abilities and helpers. This will include God's help, the presence of the Holy Spirit, prayer, as well as companions, teachers, the skills and abilities of the people, financial aid and such like.
3  **Trials and lessons.** The challenges we face and the things we endure shape our character. What are some of the challenges we have faced, and what has been strengthened as a result of that?
4  **Change and renewal.** The life of discipleship is one of transformation. How have we been changed? Have we had to let go of some things? What sacrifices have we made? What freedom have we gained?
5  **Blessing.** This section is not about us, but about the effect we have on others. As the Body of Christ, the Church is one of the ways in which people in the world encounter the living Christ. How have others been blessed as a result of what we have experienced and learned? What opportunities are there to bring blessing to others?

# Instructions

1  In advance, you may want to draw the timeline cycle diagram on each sheet of paper in advance, or ask someone in each group to do this at step 7.
2  Set up the room in advance, with tables for groups.
3  Explain the purpose of the exercise, emphasising that it is not just to create a timeline of what happened, but to explore what we might learn from looking at our shared history.
4  Spend some time creating a linear timeline (see 'Parish Timeline' exercise on page 99). Allow 20 minutes for this. If the group has already done this exercise, you can use the information from that, rather than repeat it – allow a few minutes for people to refresh their memory on this exercise.
5  Explain the nature of the journey cycle from the information in the facilitator's notes. You may want to draw a large version of the diagram on a flip chart or create a PowerPoint slide to illustrate this.
6  To familiarise people with the framework, use a well-known story from the Bible to illustrate this. There are a few examples at the end of this exercise; Mary's Story, Paul's Story, and the story of Moses and the Exodus, or you may want to use another. Ask people to identify elements of each of the five stages from the story. Write each element on a sticky note and attach it to the cycle diagram on the large sheet of paper. Allow 10–15 minutes for this, and then take feedback in the wider group. This should establish whether people have understood the process. When they have done this, they should take the sticky notes off the sheet of paper, ready for the next stage.

7 Returning to the linear timeline prepared in step 5, ask each group to work through the information on the timeline, and identify where it might fit on the cycle diagram. Allow 30 minutes for this.

8 Invite the groups to feedback on their reflections in the larger group. If there is time, encourage people to wander round and look at what other groups have produced.

9 Read James 1:2–4. Ask the groups to spend some time in reflection, and, if they can, to identify one trial that they can now give thanks to God for, because it has been a catalyst for learning, growth or blessing. This will take about 5 minutes. Note the feedback from the groups, and list the items for thanks on a clean flip chart sheet (or PowerPoint slide). Finish the exercise with a prayer of thanks, incorporating the things identified by each group.

# Story Example 1: Mary's Story

*Read Luke 1:26–56; Matthew 1:18–24, 2:1–11*

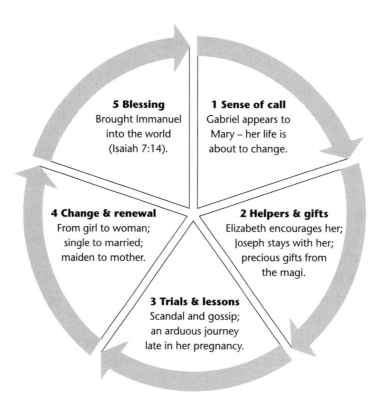

# Story Example 2: Paul's Story

*Read Acts 26:4–18, 28:17–20, 28–31*

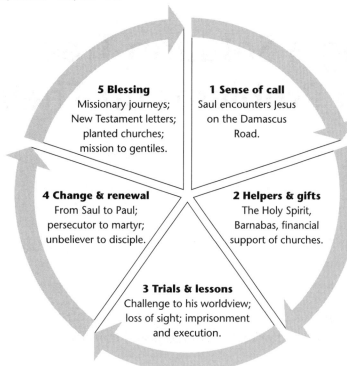

**5 Blessing**
Missionary journeys; New Testament letters; planted churches; mission to gentiles.

**1 Sense of call**
Saul encounters Jesus on the Damascus Road.

**2 Helpers & gifts**
The Holy Spirit, Barnabas, financial support of churches.

**3 Trials & lessons**
Challenge to his worldview; loss of sight; imprisonment and execution.

**4 Change & renewal**
From Saul to Paul; persecutor to martyr; unbeliever to disciple.

# Story Example 3: Moses and the Exodus

*Read: Exodus 2:11–15, 3:1–15, 4:1–17, 12:31–2*

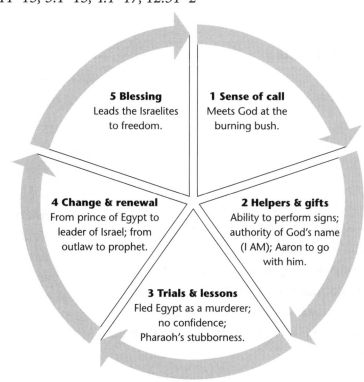

**5 Blessing**
Leads the Israelites to freedom.

**1 Sense of call**
Meets God at the burning bush.

**2 Helpers & gifts**
Ability to perform signs; authority of God's name (I AM); Aaron to go with him.

**3 Trials & lessons**
Fled Egypt as a murderer; no confidence; Pharaoh's stubborness.

**4 Change & renewal**
From prince of Egypt to leader of Israel; from outlaw to prophet.

# Growing a Solution Tree: Turning Problems on Their Heads

## Purpose

To develop a shared understanding of the causes and effects of a particular difficulty – and then to use this to identify and prioritise solutions and objectives.

## Time required

1 hour–half a day, depending on the complexity of the issue.

## Resources required

Flip chart and marker pens.

## Instructions

1 As in the 'Root Cause Analysis' activity on page 125, facilitate discussion to define the problem to be considered. This might be a difficulty that has arisen within the life of the group or congregation, or it could be an issue in the wider community, society or world that has been identified as a matter of shared concern.

2 Write the problem in the middle of the flip chart. Be as specific as possible.

> 'Looking back, the Problem Tree process is just common sense. It's kind of obvious. But it was really helpful and now we have the same understanding.'

3  Invite the group to identify direct causes and note these below the problem, joining them to the problem with a line. Then identify secondary causes (i.e., the causes of the direct causes), also linking them to the appropriate direct cause. Depending on the issue that the group is considering, it may be possible to recognise and note tertiary causes. It is important, for this activity, to express all causes in negative terms.

4  Once the causes have been exhausted, ask the group to identify effects of the problem and, if appropriate, secondary and tertiary effects. Note these above the problem as in the simplified example below.

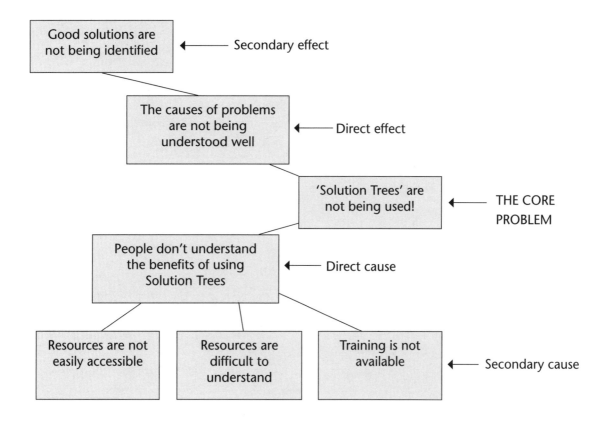

5  Develop a Solution Tree by asking people to reverse the negative statements, starting with the most indirect causes and working upwards. So, for example, negative statements that are 'secondary effects' in the example above might become: 'Resources are easily accessible', 'Resources are easy to understand' and 'Training is easily available'. This can be done by amending the Problem Tree, using a different colour pen.

6  Ask the group to identify tasks or objectives which will ensure that the Solution Tree becomes a reality. The resources available might mean that it is not be possible to implement all the solutions. In this case, invite the group to identify the objectives which will have the greatest impacts on the problem or issue.

# What next?

The Solution Tree leads to a series of positive actions. However, there are often factors and forces that work against the actions taken. 'Force Field Analysis' (on pages 144–6) is a helpful tool for understanding how forces for and against change impact the outcome. It can lead to people realising the need to augment positive actions by diminishing the forces against a change that they desire.

# Three Minutes: Share, Reflect and Pray

## Purpose

To allow individuals to speak from the heart and share something which, potentially, affects them deeply.

## Time required

15 minutes per person (for four 3-minute activities).

## Resources required

A timepiece.

## Instructions

*'When sensitively led this can deepen relationships and understanding, as well as our openness to God and one another.'*

1 Explain that each person, in turn, will have 3 minutes to share something from their recent experience, which may relate to the subject of the conversation which the group is having, or it may be something more personal. This will immediately be followed by 3 minutes when the group can ask questions related to what has been shared. Next, there will be 3 minutes when comments can be made, initially by the person who shared the experience and then by others in the group. Finally, there will be 3 minutes of prayer.
2 Repeat this four-time, 3-minute cycle with each person in turn.
3 Emphasise that you, the facilitator, will be strict with the 3-minute timing.

4  As the facilitator you may have picked up certain themes from what has been shared; be prepared to open these up with the group.
5  It is important that:
   • The facilitator who, while keeping the activity to time, is sensitive to what is being shared and the effect it is having on the group.
   • There is trust, confidence and confidentiality within the group.
   • Each person is willing to share and, potentially, to be vulnerable within the group.

## What next?

Depending upon what is shared, there may need to be personal or pastoral follow-up. This capacity must be within the group or easily available to it.

## Ideas for visuals

Nothing, unless an individual would prefer to draw their contribution.

# Asking Questions of Our Day: How to Use the Daily Examen

## Purpose

To help people reflect on their experiences and encourage awareness of the presence of God in their activity.

Using the prayer practice of Saint Ignatius of Loyola (1491–1556) called 'The Daily Examen', we look back over our day and reflect on how we chose to act. This exercise helps raise our awareness of our patterns of behaviour and how we can become more readily aware of the presence of God in our actions and in those around us. People can use this practice effectively at the end of the day to help reflect prayerfully on where they encountered God, to allow them to consolidate learning, or to start a meeting in a way that allows participants to become more aware of those around them, how they speak and act and how best to work together compassionately.

## Time required

30 minutes – depending on how you pace the reflective questions, how long you hold silence between them for people to think and reflect, or if you use an abridged version to fit with your meeting time.

## Resources required

- Suitable space and seating for people to remain quiet for the required time.
- Copy of the prayer exercise for the leader(s).

# Instructions

Ask participants to get themselves comfortable. You may wish to spend a few moments settling into the space. Ask them to sit with their feet flat on the ground and notice where their body makes contact with the chair; notice their breathing; notice how they are feeling at that particular time. From there move to explaining the process of the Daily Examen.

This prayer exercise asks questions of the day we have just lived. Looking back on our interactions with ourselves and others, we lovingly question what we have done and where we have noticed God in the midst. Be gentle and compassionate to yourself. Where you notice fault or failure, be curious, asking how you might do better tomorrow.

1  **Ask God for light: I want to look at my day with God's eyes, not merely my own.**
   - Where did my eyes linger today?
   - Where was I blind?
   - Where was I hurt without anyone noticing?
   - What did I learn today?
   - What did I read?
   - What new thoughts visited me?
   - What differences did I notice in those closest to me? Whom did I neglect?
   - Where did I neglect myself?
   - What did I begin today that might endure?

2  **Give thanks: The day I have just lived is a gift from God. I will be grateful for it.**
   - What gifts did God give me to unwrap today?
   - Where did I find encouragement? Inspiration? Hope? Compassion?
   - What stories did I have the opportunity to share?
   - What stories was I privileged to hear?

3  **Review the day: I carefully look back on the day just completed, being guided by the Holy Spirit.**
   - Where could I have exposed myself to the risk of something different?
   - Where did I allow myself to receive love?
   - With whom today did I feel the most myself?
   - What reached me today? How deep did it imprint?
   - Who saw me today?
   - Where was I aware of God's presence?
   - Where did God seem to be absent?

4  **Face your shortcomings: I face up to what is wrong – in my life and in me.**
   - What invitations was I afraid to accept?
   - Where did I trespass?
   - Who do I need to forgive?
   - Who do I need to ask for forgiveness?
   - What do I need to let go?

5  **Look toward the day to come.**
   - What do I need to carry with me from today?
   - What do I need to lay down?

## Close the Examen with this prayer:

God, show me what is important or significant from today that will shape tomorrow.

God, help me to recognise what is merely a distraction.

God, open our eyes to what is in front of us, in the light of this, and help us to walk the road you have called us to travel.

# Deepening Understanding: God, Ourselves and Our Community

## Purpose

To help, in an ongoing way, evaluate a project and understand better what people are learning.

This activity is particularly appropriate for individuals and small groups (2–6). If used in a larger group, then it can be for individual reflection, or, if the larger group breaks into pairs, triplets or smaller groups, for group reflection. Keeping a record of responses (individual and group) over time can be both instructive and encouraging.

## Time required

Time is, in part, dependent on the size of the group, but to go beyond 60–90 minutes is likely, in most cases, to give diminishing returns.

## Resources required

- Pen and paper for individuals.
- Flip chart and paper if group wish to collate responses and later record them.

# Instructions

1 The purpose of this exercise is to help us, in a structured yet conversational way, evaluate a project, deepen our understanding and discern the next step.
2 The exercise is based around a series of five simple questions (see below for questions). Each question is looked at in turn.
3 Begin by taking a few moments of personal reflection on Question 1, and then discuss this together. We intentionally begin with focusing on our relationship with God, as too often when evaluating projects we only think of activity (rather than the relationships which give rationale and foundation to our actions).
4 Collate the key points on the flip chart.
5 Repeat the process with Questions 2 to 5.
6 With Question 4 the group should not be under any pressure to provide answers as the reflecting on these uncertainties might be part of the next step. It is, however, important, in Question 5, that a next step (or series of steps) is agreed and that the group holds itself accountable to this.

## Questions

Since we last met:

1 What have I/we (as a church community and/or whatever groupings that are represented) learnt about God?
2 What have I/we learnt about myself/ourselves (as a church community and/or whatever groupings are represented)?
3 What have I/we learnt about our wider community?
4 Have I/we any questions?
5 What is the next step (or series of steps)?

# What next?

The frequency of this type of evaluation/developing understanding can vary, depending on the group and the nature of the project in which they are involved. However, at set intervals, perhaps after every three to four evaluations, the group can look back and see how they and the project have developed.

# Ideas for visuals

Symbols can be used instead of questions (as in the Swedish method of Bible Study, upon which this is based), e.g.

↑       God

→       Self/Church Community

?       Question

!       To do

→→      Wider Community

# SWOT Analysis:
# Strengths, Weaknesses, Opportunities and Threats

## Purpose

To help a group assess a situation, context or project and to begin to discern the next step forward.

This activity uses four simple categories:

- Strengths: what are the identifiable strengths of what is being considered?
- Weaknesses: what are the identifiable weaknesses?
- Opportunities: from the identified strengths, what potential opportunities are apparent?
- Threats (if the term 'Threats' sounds too negative 'Challenges' can be used): from the identified weaknesses or challenges, what might hinder the potential opportunities from being realised?

Although there is a realistic appraisal of weaknesses and threats, the overall focus is on assets and opportunities and how these may be optimised.

## Time required

1½–2 hours.

## Resources required

- A facilitator who is familiar with SWOT analysis and how to develop a focused conversation from this.
- Flip chart.
- Marker pens (various colours).

# Instructions

1 Explain to the group what a SWOT analysis is.
2 Together the group identifies 'Strengths'. Ask people to say what comes to mind and encourage lateral thinking. Don't rush this stage.
3 The facilitator writes each word/phrase on the flip chart page(s) headed 'Strengths'.
4 When all has been said, quickly recap, identify themes, and ask for people's reaction to list.
5 Repeat process for 'Weaknesses'.
6 Now consider the 'Opportunities' category. Ask for suggestions based on the strengths which have been identified. Give time for people to engage with this link and to be creative; encourage comments or short discussion, though don't lose sight of your overall timescale.
7 Repeat process for 'Threats/Challenges'.
8 Help the group to discuss their observations as a whole (putting the 4 flip charts sheets up on a 2x2 grid might be helpful) and then encourage them, from the insights gained, to decide on a 'next step' (no matter how small). This stage is important, as analysis without a way forward can be frustrating and potentially dispiriting for a group.

# What next?

Agree how to put the 'next step' into action; this should include responsibilities and time scale. Then agree when to meet to evaluate the results of the 'next step', so that momentum will not be lost.

# Ideas for visuals

Be prepared for people to respond in images – draw these (even badly), or have someone lined up to do so.

# Root Cause Analysis:
# Getting beyond Quick Fixes

## Purpose

To understand problems or difficulties better, to dig down to the root causes and to develop some solutions.

Root Cause Analysis does this by using facilitated conversations to define the problem, collect data/evidence, determine possible causal factors, identify root causes and agree strategies for overcoming the problem. Involving a group of people in this exercise will help gain a richer understanding than is possible for any individual, more creative solutions can be considered and there is greater likelihood that these people will own decisions that proceed from this activity and be part of the solution.

## Time required

40 minutes–2 hours, depending on the size of the group and the complexity of the issue.

## Resources required

- Flip chart with a simple diagram of a tree with roots, branches, small branches and leaves or fruit.
- Marker pens.

# Instructions

1 With the flip chart in clear view of all participants, the facilitator explains that the first stage of this activity is to define the problem. Introduce some ground rules that ensure that everyone is able to contribute. Having given a brief and non-judgemental introduction to the matter under discussion, invite people to contribute to defining the problem by sharing their insights on 'What can we see that is evidence of this problem?' and 'What are some symptoms of this problem?' Write contributions on or beside the leaves or fruit of the tree.

2 Examine the problem by collecting some background data, by asking 'How long has the problem existed?' and 'What are some of the impacts of the problem?' Record answers on or beside the branches of the tree.

3 Identify possible causal factors, by asking 'What other problems are associated with the main issue?'; 'What are the conditions that enable the problem to occur?'; 'Was there a sequence of events that led to this problem?' Write answers on the trunk of the tree.

4 Now it is time to dig deeper. For each causal factor, ask the question 'Why?' several times – until you establish a root cause (see diagram below). It is important to know when to stop. Ask the question 'Is this a root cause or should we be asking "Why?" once more?' Write the root causes in or beside the roots of the tree on the flip chart. Make a final check that there are no root causes that have been missed.

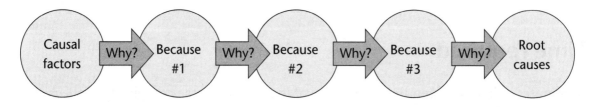

5 Invite suggestions for solutions and record these on a clean page of the flip chart. With this page and the tree diagram side by side, check that the suggested actions will resolve the problem and prevent it happening again. Clarify what action will be taken, how, who is responsible, what resources are needed, what risks are involved and how they can be mitigated, and how and when the action will be evaluated.

# Section 6
# DISCERNING OUR FUTURE

# Introduction

We are living through a period of extraordinary change. Observers in various fields of study believe that this present time is not only an 'era of change', but displays all the hallmarks of a 'change of era'. In other words, shifts in society at every level are so far-reaching that we are witnessing an epoch-defining season of social and technological transformation. In a context of such fluidity and flux, it is unsurprising that, in the worlds of business, health care and education, 'strategic planning' is recognised as vital. For commercial enterprises and service providers alike, the challenges involved in continuing to be relevant, effective and efficient, are significant; continuous reappraisal and learning is crucial; 'business as usual' is not an option. Being alert to trends within society and predicting future needs or fashions are vital. Organisational flexibility and the ability of people to adapt and thrive through times of transition are essential if organisations are to survive and flourish.

But what about the Church? Some might argue that, in the churn and chaos of such colossal change, the Church should provide stability and predictability, a safe harbour from the storm. After all, the Lord is our rock (Ps. 18:2); the one we follow is 'the same yesterday and today and forever' (Heb. 13:8). However, when we read our Bibles and review the history of the Church, we find that our 'never-changing God' calls us to be observant and attentive of 'the signs of the times' and wise as we use our gifts and resources for the extension of God's kingdom. While our future is most definitely in God's hands (Ps. 31:15), that is not an excuse for fatalistic inactivity; it is not an instruction to simply trust the Lord and do nothing. The notion that ostriches 'bury their head in the sand' when facing danger has been thoroughly debunked. The idea that our 'never-changing God' desires a 'never-changing Church' is, likewise, a myth – and an unhelpful one.

If, ignoring the changes occurring in our context, we plan to do exactly the same in the future as we have done in the past, we will soon become relevant to a situation that no longer exists. By 'relevant', nobody is suggesting that the Church should uncritically embrace every fad and fashion or allow contemporary culture to squeeze us into its mould. Rather, we need to discern how we are to live and proclaim the Gospel afresh in our generation. Throughout history, the Church, its worship and mission have taken many forms and expressions – as the unchanging Gospel has encountered different cultures at particular times in history.

As we prayerfully seek God's vision for our congregations and groups, we become part of the exciting and challenging process of being the Church, which, as the leaders of the Protestant Reformation declared, is 'reformed and always being reformed'. Without engaging in processes of discerning what it is that God wants *us* to be and do, without re-envisioning Church in our particular situation, we run the risk of finding ourselves disconnected from the wider community and answering questions that nobody is asking. Over time, a frustrating disconnection and a cultural gulf will develop between the life of the congregation or group and the rest of life; involvement will no longer equip, inspire and energise members for being disciples in those areas of life where they spend most of their time.

The activities in this section have been found to be helpful in enabling people to share their unique perspectives and experiences as they, together, discern what God might be revealing to them. There are activities here which, when used sensitively and prayerfully, will aid your congregation or group to find fresh vision for the future. While some leaders may be apprehensive of encouraging the widest participation possible in the matter of vision and future planning, the activities detailed here help to develop a truly *shared* vision, building ownership and commitment along the way. Indeed, experience of using these exercises is that God often uses consensus around particular ideas and thoughts as a way of guiding and inspiring.

Far from being irreverent, expecting that God uses all kinds of means to show us the way forward is entirely consistent with what we know of God's character and purposes. As Jesus explained to his first disciples, 'I no longer call you servants, because a servant does not know his master's business. Instead, I have called you friends, for everything that I learned from my Father I have made known to you' (John 15:15). As his disciples in this generation, with a responsibility towards the generations to come, learning to listen and discern our future *together* is vital.

# Letter to the Eighth Church: Seeking a Christ's Eye View

## Purpose

To reflect on how Jesus might see our group or congregation in order to highlight strengths to build on and areas of challenge that require attention. To grow a shared perspective on the health and direction of the group or church as participants share their insights with one another.

## Time required

90 minutes–2 hours.

There can be benefit in splitting this activity into two sessions of about 1 hour each: one in which people draft their letters; a second one when people share their letters and the facilitator builds up a picture from the different contributions. Having time between these two aspects of the exercise gives people the opportunity for deeper reflection and a chance to further develop their insights before sharing with others.

## Resources required

- Bibles.
- Pre-prepared sheets of A4 paper with the appropriate headings on both front and back (see right).
- Pens.
- Flip chart.
- Marker pens.
- Chairs arranged around tables in groups of 3–5, with sufficient papers and pens on each table.

| |
|---|
| Name of church |
| A title for Christ |
| A commendation |
| A critique |
| A challenge |
| A promise |
| A call to listen to the Spirit |

# Instructions

1 Invite people to turn in their Bibles to the book of Revelation. Explain that the opening chapters of Revelation picture the Risen Christ moving among his churches. In chapters 2 and 3 he sends a letter to each of the seven churches of Asia. Highlight the fact that each of these letters follows a similar format. There is a title for Christ which acts as a kind of touchstone for their life as a church. This is followed, in each case, by a commendation, a critique, a challenge, a promise and finally, a call to listen to the Spirit. Draw attention to each of these in the letter to the Church in Ephesus (Rev. 2:1–7).

2 Allocate each group one of the remaining six letters and ask them to (quite quickly) review the letter and then note its content on the front of their sheet of paper under the headings. Allow 10 minutes for this part of the activity.

3 Ask each group to turn their sheet of paper over and to consider what the Risen Christ would want to say to their congregation or group. Give a few minutes for each person to consider this quietly. Then invite them to spend about 10 minutes having a conversation in their small group regarding this. Then ask them to consider their thoughts carefully and prayerfully and record them under each heading on the sheet.

4 In plenary session, with a flip chart in clear view, starting with 'A commendation', request people to review what they have written and ask them, 'If you were to summarise in 1 or 2 words what it is that the Risen Christ would say "Well done" about, what would they be?' Record all responses on the flip chart. If people say the same or similar things, this can be reflected on the flip chart with a number of ticks.

5 Using a new sheet on the flip chart for each heading, work through them in a similar fashion, leaving the 'A title for Christ' until last.

> 'Quite challenging. It was like applying the "What would Jesus do?" idea to our congregation. Some good things came out of it and I think we were all surprised at the agreement that came out at the end.'

# What next?

When the group has reviewed the portrait which emerges from the above process, ask participants to react to the challenge, 'Listen to what the Spirit says to the church', by noting possible responses using the 'Traffic Lights' framework (things to stop, things to change, discuss, consider or things to start) in the 'Where Do We Start?' activity on page 138. You can then use the 'Clustering' exercise in the 'Dreaming Dreams' activity on page 133 to discern whether there is consensus around certain suggestions.

# Cool Wall: Mapping Trends and How they Affect the Church

## Purpose

To look at what outside factors influence church culture and consider the appropriate response.

Culture shifts and changes over time, with trends (defined as 'a general direction in which something is developing or changing') appearing and disappearing – often at great pace. But beyond the zeitgeist, there is lasting change that can have significant impact on such things as how we behave, our mobility, our sense of national identity, or how we engage with technology.

The Church is not only affected by these trends, but can either influence change or disconnect and become seemingly irrelevant in the midst of these changes.

- How then, as the Church, should we recognise and respond to changing cultures and trends?
- Which changes appear to be more 'fads' than part of a significant trend?
- Should we be in step with the changes, or should we be counter-cultural in our response?

This exercise helps us to look at changes in culture, recognise and talk about the impact of trends that have become evident in our lives and consider if we are in tune with them, out of step or unaware.

## Time required

90 minutes–2 hours.

## Resources required

- 1 roll of newsprint paper / lining paper / the reverse side of left-over wallpaper.
- 1 pen for each participant.

## Instructions

1  Using a large sheet of paper, ask a volunteer to draw a timeline ranging from +5 years, NOW, -5 years, -10 years to -20 years
   - Invite the whole group to take 15 minutes to brainstorm ideas about changes in culture or trends that you have recognised or remember. Everyone should have a pen so that they can write their ideas on the timeline without having to use one person as a scribe. This will ensure the maximum number of ideas can be noted. You will be discussing each trend later, so it is best to keep things moving and encourage people to write without too much discussion at this stage.
   - Take 15 minutes to decide on the most significant changes.
2  Choose five trends and split them between several smaller groups.
   Take 30 minutes to discuss these trends in the small groups. These prompts may be helpful for the discussions:
   - What are the positives and negatives of each trend?
   - How does this change affect the community?
   - How does this change affect the most affluent?
   - How does this change affect the most vulnerable?
3  Take 30 minutes to look at the +5 years section of the timeline and brainstorm ideas about what trends are emerging or what cultural changes might be on the horizon.
   It may be helpful to ask:
   - What, if any, of these emerging trends should the church engage with?
   - What seems to be more like a fad rather than a change of any considerable depth?
   - What changes might the church itself have to make to respond to this change?
4  Take time to discuss what felt valuable from the session.
5  Close in prayer, particularly asking for discernment.

## What next?

Are there groups that would benefit from this information/process, such as the elders or groups with a focus on outreach and mission?

# Dreaming Dreams: Starting to Discern a Vision

## Purpose

To encourage people to dream dreams (no matter how unrealistic) for approximately two to three years' ahead and enable small groups to narrow down what might be a vast number of individual dreams into three main priority dream themes, which, in turn, will help in the process of discerning a vision for the congregation as a whole.

As part of an envisioning process, it is important to allow people, through the Holy Spirit's inspiration, to dream dreams. However, when such an exercise is run, there may be a tendency for those involved to imagine what they think *will* happen, as opposed to what they *want* to see happen. Such an aspirational exercise is known in business terminology as 'blue sky thinking'.

## Time required

1 hour maximum.

## Resources required

- Large sheets of paper (e.g. lining paper).
- Sticky notes.
- Pens.
- Flip chart easel with paper.
- Marker pens.

# Instructions

1 In preparation, cut out the required number of strips of lining paper, each approximately one and a half metres long. Between 20 and 25cm (about nine inches) in from the right hand end of the paper, use a bold marker pen to draw a dotted line from the top to the bottom of the paper. This will leave an end section for a subsequent exercise. At the top end of this section write the title, 'Hopes, Vision, Dreams'.

2 Arrange for those attending to be seated around tables in small groups. Ensure every table has a large sheet of paper, prepared in advance as described above. Also ensure there are enough ballpoint pens for everyone and at least one whole sticky notepad (100 sheets) per table.

3 Introduce the topic and then ask any of the following questions to help people in their thinking:

  • If you travelled forward in time by two or three years in Dr Who's Tardis and the door opens, what would you love to see in your church and/or the community?

  • Imagine you are in (name of year) and you see a newspaper headline regarding your church. What headline would you love to read?

  • Imagine you are in (name of year) and you are queueing in the local post office, over-hearing a conversation about your church. What would you love to hear?

  • In two or three years' time, how would you like your church to be known in the community – especially by those with no church connection?

4 Invite each person to have as many dreams as they wish, but to write only one dream on each sticky note. This is important for the next part of the exercise. Dreams may be related to the church, the community, or both. Encourage everyone to write whatever they individually wish – be it new organ pipes or the whole community coming to faith. They then place the sticky notes down anywhere on the large sheet of paper except for the end section marked 'Hopes, Vision, Dreams'. Try to discourage any discussion at this point.

# CLUSTERING: GRADUALLY SEEING THE BIGGER PICTURE

*This part of the exercise can stand alone as an activity to be used across a number of themes, but in this case, is an important continuation of the above process. If taken alone, the time required would be 30 minutes maximum.*

## Instructions

5  Ensure all materials remain in place, but also provide a set of marker pens for each group. Invite each group now to work together and to 'cluster' the dreams into similar ideas, such as all those concerning young people, those concerning worship, those concerning fabric and finance matters, etc.

6  The clustering may take on the form of 'ladders', where sticky notes are stuck together in columns. This is a good, space-saving technique, but feel free to permit the groups to use their own methods.

7  As with the previous part of the exercise, encourage each group to keep the end section of their sheet of paper marked 'Hopes, Vision, Dreams' clear of any sticky notes while clustering.

8  Some sticky notes may have dreams that don't relate to any others. That does not make them any less valid and clusters of just one or two are perfectly acceptable.

9  After about 10 minutes, check all groups are satisfied with their clusters and explain that as people look at the clusters, the size of some of them may be significant, but perhaps some of the most 'pointed' dreams may be those grouped on their own. In other words, size is not necessarily most important.

10  Invite the groups to look at their clusters and from them, agree on the three most important dreams for the future. Once a consensus is reached, invite each group to write them in the end section of their sheet of paper with a marker pen.

11  Invite the groups to look at their three key dreams and to agree on which of them is the most important of all and to underline or circle it with a marker pen.

12  Finally, invite each group to read out their dreams, starting with their 'top dream' and write them up on the flip chart. When all groups have fed back their dreams, it should be possible to see if there are common dreams or themes. It is highly likely that from, say, four groups offering three dreams each, totalling twelve, as few as three or four 'dream themes' may be evident.

## What next?

See the 'Where do We Start?' activity on page 138.

# What Do You Want?
# Imagining the Future of
# Our Church

## Purpose

To imagine the best possible future for our church, without being hampered by definitions of success.

This is an appreciative process, which utilises some of the principles of Lectio Divina (see 'Reading between the Lines' on page 21) allowing reflection on Scripture to be the starting point for envisioning a future for the church. It works best in small groups so that as many people as possible have the opportunity to actively participate, sharing stories and encouraging one another.

## Time required

About 1 hour.

## Resources required

- Paper for writing notes.
- 1 pen for each participant.
- 1 Bible.

# Instructions

1 Arrange people in small groups. Invite them to take 1 minute each to discuss an initial question which will frame the session: 'What is the brightest, or highest, future you want to see for the church?' (This might be local, global, denominational, in the context of the community, for example, but should be made clear at the outset.) When asking this framing question, avoid using language which implies success or failure, such as 'successful', 'thriving', 'best' or such like.

2 Now ask people to share a story of when they had a meaningful experience of God. People should not feel pressurised into doing this, but as many as feel able should have the opportunity to do so. Again, be careful of the language in the question – allow participants to self-define what 'meaningful' means – it is important that no-one feels as though they are being judged. Allow 10 minutes for this.

3 Invite someone to read the story of blind Bartimaeus from the Bible, Mark 10:46–52, then ask: 'If this was the only story we had in Scripture, what would we say God was like?' Allow 10 minutes for this.

4 Ask someone else to read out the same story for a second time, Mark 10:46–52. Give participants some time to journal in private, using the paper and pens provided, considering what their response would be if Jesus asked them, 'What is it that you want me to do for you?' Allow 5 minutes for this.

5 Ask a third person to read the story, this time a shortened version, Mark 10:48–51. This focuses the reading on Jesus' question. Ask people to discuss how they would respond if Jesus asked them, 'What is it that you want me to do for the church?' Allow about 5 minutes for this.

6 Ask someone to read again the question Jesus asks in Mark 10:51. Invite small groups to join up into larger groups of 6–8 and discuss: 'What do you want Jesus to do for this community?' Allow 15 minutes for this.

7 Repeat the framing question used at the beginning: 'What is the brightest, or highest, future you want to see for the church?' Take some feedback from the whole group on this.

8 Finally, ask people to journal for 1–2 minutes about what has stood out for them from this session. Has it been worthwhile? What have they particularly noticed? Allow a few minutes for feedback in the whole group.

# Variations

To reduce the time required for this activity, the Bible reading may be read just once, at step 3.

# Where Do We Start? Setting Priorities

## Purpose

To prioritise the most effective way of beginning the journey towards any discerned vision or collection of dreams.

Below are two easy-to-use alternative exercises for helping to prioritise measures that may help a congregation move forward to those dreams. A third exercise ('Voting') is suggested as a way of helping to reach a consensus.

## EXERCISE A – IMPACT VERSUS COST

## Time required

Approximately 50 minutes (up to 90 minutes if including 'Voting' exercise).

## Resources required

- A list of the main dreams agreed by each group from the 'Dreaming Dreams' exercise.
- Flip chart easel with paper.
- Extra flip chart sheets (1 sheet per group).
- Marker pens.
- Sticky notes.

# Instructions

'You might not do everything you talk about, but if you can identify from the ideas presented what's possible and what isn't, that's a good thing.'

1 Invite people to form small groups, seated around tables ('café style') and provide each group with a list of the main dreams (one A4 sheet of paper should suffice), a piece of flip chart paper, marker pens and sticky notes.

2 Ask each group to use their marker pens to draw a simple, four-square grid that more or less fills the sheet of paper. At the top of the top-right square, ask the groups to write the heading 'High Impact – Low Cost'. At the top of the top-left square, ask them to write the heading 'High Impact – High Cost'. For the lower left square, ask them to put the heading 'Low Impact – Low Cost', and for the lower right square, the heading 'Low Impact – High Cost'. The matrix should look similar to this:

| High Impact – Low Cost | High Impact – High Cost |
|---|---|
| Low Impact – Low Cost | Low Impact – High Cost |

3 Invite each group, using the list of key dreams, to agree on new measures or objectives that they feel will be steps along the journey towards the dreams. These are to be written onto individual sticky notes (one measure per sticky note), which are then to be stuck onto the sheet, but in no particular place.

4 Explain the meaning of the grid's four headings. The *High Impact – Low Cost* box/square represents those measures that, if accomplished, would have a significant (positive) impact, but require relatively little in terms of money, time or other resources. These are often referred to as 'quick wins'. The *High Impact – High Cost* square represents those measures that again, would have a significant impact, but require considerable money, time and resources. These would be more long-term in nature and are often referred to as 'strategic'. The *Low Impact – Low Cost* square represents those measures that would have little impact, but don't require much in terms of money, time or resources. These are often referred to as 'debatable'. Finally, the *Low Impact – High Cost* square represents those measures that would have little impact, but require a lot of input, whether in money, time or other resources. These are probably best to avoid altogether, or at the most, be given the lowest priority.

5 Invite each group to look at their sticky notes and agree on where each measure should be placed on the grid.

6 After allowing appropriate time for debate and decisions within the groups, invite spokespersons from the groups to feed back their choices and write up on the flip chart those chosen for the top two squares (those with 'High Impact').

7 With agreement from the groups, delete any obvious duplication, to leave a distinct list of separate new measures.

8 There may well be a good number of suggested measures and it would be impractical to attempt them all. Explain that concentrating energy on a few areas of activity is almost always a more rewarding approach. Clarify to the groups the need to agree on prioritising a smaller number of measures that are believed to be most effective.

## What next?

See the 'Voting' exercise to help everyone gain a consensus on what measures to prioritise.

# EXERCISE B – TRAFFIC LIGHTS

## Time required

About 50 minutes (up to 90 minutes if including 'Voting' exercise).

## Resources required

- List of the main dreams agreed by each group from the 'Dreaming Dreams' exercise.
- Flip chart easel with paper.
- Extra flip chart sheets (1 sheet per group).
- Marker pens.
- Sticky notes.

# Instructions

1  Invite people to form small groups, seated around tables ('café style') and provide each group with a list of the main dreams (one A4 sheet of paper should suffice), a piece of flip chart paper, marker pens and sticky notes.

2  Invite each group to use a marker pen to divide their sheet of paper into three sections (it does not matter whether it is laid out in 'landscape' or 'portrait' style).

3  Invite the groups to write 'Red', 'Amber' and 'Green' at the top of the three sections. The sheets should now look similar to this:

| Red |
| --- |
| Amber |
| Green |

4  Invite each group to use the list of key dreams and agree on new measures or objectives that they feel will be steps along the journey towards the dreams. These are to be written onto individual sticky notes (one measure per sticky note). Furthermore, invite the groups to write on sticky notes all their current church activities (again, one per sticky note). All of the sticky notes are then to be stuck onto the sheet, but in no particular place.

5  Explain the meanings of the three sections. The 'red' section represents all those current activities which the group agrees should be stopped, or at least put into abeyance in order that people, resources and/or funds can be re-allocated to more beneficial activities or measures elsewhere. There may even be some suggested new measures that are not considered effective and so they also end up in this section. The 'amber' section represents any current activities or suggested new measures that the group agrees are more 'open to discussion'. On the one hand they may be considered useful in progressing towards the dreams, but alternatively, they may not be considered as top priority. They may need further discussion or may be considered for undertaking, but require particular groundwork or preparation. The 'green' section represents not only those current activities that are agreed to be maintained and even developed, but also those new measures that are agreed will be worth undertaking as soon as possible. In each case, agreement is based upon the notion that the activities or new measures will be most effective in progressing towards the dreams.

6  Invite the groups to look at all their sticky notes and agree on where each should be placed within the three sections: 'red', 'amber' or 'green'.

7   After allowing appropriate time for debate and decisions within the groups, invite spokespersons from the groups to feed back their choices and write up on the flip chart those chosen for the 'amber' and 'green' sections only.

8   With agreement from the groups, delete any obvious duplication, to leave a distinct list of separate activities and new measures.

9   There may well be a good number of activities and measures, but it would be impractical to attempt them all. Explain that concentrating energy on a few areas of activity is almost always a more rewarding approach. Clarify to the groups the need to agree on prioritising a smaller number of measures that are believed to be most effective, that is, those items offered from the 'green' sections.

## What next?

See the 'Voting' exercise to help everyone gain a consensus on what activities and new measures to prioritise.

# VOTING – REACHING A CONSENSUS ON PRIORITIES

## Purpose

To follow up either the 'Impact versus Cost' or the 'Traffic Lights' exercise.

A swift way of reaching 'the wisdom in the room' is to vote on the preferred measures suggested. It is a simple exercise, but also a flexible one, depending for example, on choosing the number of votes to be agreed upon.

## Time required

About 30 minutes (more time is needed for larger groups).

## Resources required

- Flip chart easel with paper.
- Sheets of sticky dots (approximately 1 cm in diameter).

# Instructions

1 Write up the feedback from the above exercises with a clear space between items.

2 Ensure each person has a small number of sticky dots. The dots are usually sold in packs with many dots arranged on several small backing sheets and it is easy to cut strips of say four or five for distribution. They are very easy to peel off when needed. The colour of the dots is not particularly relevant.

3 Explain that each person has (for this example) three votes and therefore has three sticky dots. Invite everybody to look at the items listed on the flip chart and consider for themselves as individuals (no discussion allowed) which three they would prefer to see undertaken.

4 Invite everyone to come forward (you may wish to organise this in an informal way, such as over a comfort break, in order to minimise the self-consciousness of some individuals) and place each of their sticky dots next to the items of their choice.

5 Encourage people to make up their minds before approaching the flip chart. This will help to guard against a tendency for those further back in the queue to look at the numbers of dots against more popular items and then 'go with the flow' and add yet more dots to them.

6 After everyone has had the opportunity to cast their (e.g. three) votes, count the number of sticky dots next to each item. It is highly likely that popular items will emerge, but in this example, the three items with the highest numbers of sticky dots are being sought.

7 Using this example, the three items receiving the most votes may be considered those to treat with the highest priority and therefore targeted for where most energy needs to be directed.

# What next?

It will depend on the groups undertaking the exercise, but generally, the results of the voting will help determine how to move forward. As with all priorities, it is a matter of degrees and it should be stressed that those items receiving a lower vote need not be scrapped, but simply be given less priority than those scoring highest.

# Force Field Analysis: Understanding and Managing Forces for and against Change

## Purpose

To develop an understanding of the different factors and influences which combine to make change possible or ensure that the status quo remains.

Drawing on the collective wisdom of all, this activity enhances decision making. By making forces for and against change explicit, it helps identify ways of implementing change more effectively.

## Time required

40–90 minutes, depending on the size of the group and the complexity of the issue.

## Resources required

- Flip chart.
- Marker pens.

## Instructions

1 It is useful if people understand the foundations of the techniques used in this activity. Here is a brief background:

Kurt Lewin (1890–1947) was a pioneering psychologist with a particular interest in human behaviour and change. His ideas are striking in their simplicity and profound in their insight and influence. He observed that, when effective change takes place in human groups of any size, a three-stage process occurs. He expressed this in terms of 'unfreezing–changing–refreezing'. 'Unfreezing' refers to the necessity of building awareness of the need for change and recognising that the status quo should not continue. 'Changing' involves building consensus for the new. People need to understand the reasons for change and be able to imagine the benefits. Once new ways of being and/or doing become reality, it is important to ensure that the changes are thoroughly incorporated and become the new normal. This is 'refreezing'. During this phase

> *'Until we worked through that exercise none of us had the whole picture. Now we have the same understanding and we've been able to see some ways in which we can help our plans become reality.'*

people become comfortable with the new and confident in any changes in their own roles. When we understand change within our congregation or group in these terms it is easy to grasp that, at any particular time, things change or stay the same because of competing forces: forces for change and forces for sameness. For a particular change to happen, the factors that are pro that change need to be greater than the forces and influences which are resisting change. Kurt Lewin suggested a simple method to help people better understand the opposing forces in relation to a potential change so that, firstly, they can make good decisions and, secondly, they can increase the likelihood of effective change occurring. Since it was first developed in the 1940s, his 'Force Field Analysis' tool has been widely used in all kinds of organisations, including churches.

2  Introduce and agree the area of potential change that is under consideration.

3  Create a Force Field Analysis template on the flip chart, easily visible for all participants and write the title of the matter under discussion in a column in the centre of the page. Add a column heading to its left titled 'Forces FOR Change' and a column heading to its right with the title 'Forces AGAINST Change'.

Forces FOR Change                Forces AGAINST Change

Potential change under consideration

4 Invite participants to identify as many reasons or forces *for* the potential change as possible and note these on the left of the flip chart. In the same way, encourage people to recognise as many reasons or forces *against* the potential change as possible, recording these to the right.

5 Ask participants to consider the degree of influence each factor has on the potential change, using a simple rating system, from 1 (weak) to 5 (strong), and then add up the scores for each side (for and against). You can enhance the visual impact of this by drawing arrows around each influence, using bigger arrows for greater influence and smaller ones for weaker ones.

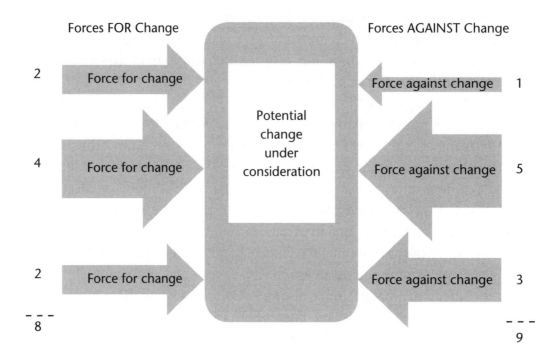

6 The group can now use this visual representation in two ways: to decide whether to move ahead with the potential change and, if so, to consider how to strengthen the supportive forces and how to minimise the resisting forces, thus optimising the chances of effective change.

# Why Mission?
# Exploring What Motivates Us for Mission

## Purpose

To help us to understand better what motivates people to get involved in mission, in order to encourage better everyone in our congregations or other groups to support the church's work in mission.

## Time required

50 minutes–1 hour.

## Resources required

- Flip chart.
- Marker pens.
- Paper for making notes.
- 1 pen for each participant.
- Sticky notes.

## Instructions

1 Arrange people in groups around tables and explain the purpose of the exercise. As a short connecting-up exercise, ask people to share with the person next to them what motivated them to attend this session. This should only take a few minutes.

2 Ask the groups to list some of the activities that their church engages in, and record them on the flip chart sheet. Take some feedback from the groups, and display their flip chart sheets on a wall or display board, so that everyone can see them. Allow 7–8 minutes for this.

3 Invite the groups to pick two of the activities listed – it can be from their own list or another group's. If possible, pick one that at least some in the group are involved in, and one that at least some are not involved in. Ask the groups to consider the following questions:
   • For an activity you are involved in, what are your reasons for being involved?
   • For an activity you are not involved in, why not, and what would motivate you to get involved?

   Encourage people to be honest. This exercise is not designed to test whether people understand the 'correct' answers – it is to discover what truly encourages people. Participants should write their responses on sticky notes – one motivational factor per note. Allow 10–15 minutes for this.

4 Take feedback from all the groups. Ask one group at a time to bring their sticky notes to the front. Read them out as you stick them to a flip chart or display board. As each group adds their notes, cluster similar ones into groups as you go along. There should be a range of factors, perhaps including biblical instructions, compassion, or because it creates a benefit for those we care about.

5 Ask participants to reflect on what they have learned about why people engage in mission, and how they can motivate others to get involved. Allow about 10 minutes for people to discuss this in their groups.

6 Finish with a time of open discussion, asking what practical steps people can take to share a vision for mission with others.

# If There was One Thing?
# Small Steps to Meaningful Change

## Purpose

To identify some possible changes that individuals and congregations or groups can make quickly, and some bigger ideas to pray about and consider.

To enable quick wins, and engender ownership and personal engagement among participants. To demonstrate that small changes can make a big difference, and can be achieved without necessarily requiring large investment of resources or time.

To encourage each participant to make a commitment to making at least one change.

The exercise begins with a focus on individual change, as in order to create change, we must be willing to change ourselves. It develops to encourage a sense of ownership of what we can do as individuals to contribute to positive change on a wider scale.

## Time required

About 1 hour.

## Resources required

- Paper for making notes.
- Sticky notes.
- Flip chart, or suitable area of wall to display sticky notes.
- 1 pen for each participant.
- 1 small piece of card for each participant – postcard size is ideal.

# Facilitator notes

It may be useful to share some stories of where small changes have been beneficial. A quick search on the internet will find many stories from business and health. One useful source is the 'Small Changes, Big Difference' project from NHS Borders http://www.nhsborders. scot.nhs.uk/small-changes-big-difference, where staff and patients were asked to share their stories about small changes that have benefited their health.

# Instructions

1  Arrange participants in groups around tables, equipped with paper, pens and sticky notes.
2  As a connecting-up exercise, ask participants to turn to the person next to them, and share about a time when they made a simple change to their own wellbeing, their discipleship or the life of the church, which was beneficial.
3  To familiarise the participants with the process of this exercise, ask them to chat to their neighbours for a few minutes about an aspect of their life they would like to change, for example, health and fitness, learning something new, having more time for family or friends, decluttering their home and such like.
4  Once the participants have identified something, ask everyone to work on their own to list all the changes they could make in their lives to achieve this. It is important to stress that the purpose is not to find a single solution that would wholly achieve their aims, but to list as many things as possible that would make some difference to the situation, however small. Allow 5 minutes for this. Now ask everyone to highlight *one* that is in their power to implement, and can be easily achieved. Invite them to consider that, while this will not make things perfect, it may improve the situation.
5  Now ask everyone to think about their life of discipleship. What would they like to change – what might deepen their relationship with God, or help them to live out their faith? Allow time for people to journal in private, using the paper provided. As before, ask everyone to select one thing they might want to change and to list all the things they could do that would help achieve that. Allow 5 minutes for this. When they have done this, again, invite them to highlight just one that they can implement easily.
6  The next steps are for group discussion. Ask the groups to list ten good things about their church. Allow 5 minutes for this, and ask for feedback from each group on one or two things on their list. This is an important step, as without it the following discussion can quickly become negative and critical.
7  Ask the groups to consider what would make their good church even better, and to list them on sticky notes, with each item on a separate note, and place them in the centre of their table or workspace.

8  Ask individuals to choose one of the ideas, and consider what they could do to help bring this about. It doesn't matter if several people choose the same item. Invite them to consider what part they might play in creating the desired change, and to list all the ideas they can, only including ideas that they can personally take responsibility for. For example, the desired outcome may be that the church is more welcoming. Rather than a solution which depends on other people, such as 'training for the Welcome Team', a personal response might be, 'I will make a point of talking to visitors to the church.' Allow about 5 minutes for this.

9  When everyone has had a chance to do this, ask people to share just one of their ideas with their group. This will take about 10–15 minutes.

10  Give everyone a small piece of card, and invite them to write on it:
   • 'One thing I will do to enhance my personal wellbeing is [complete this sentence from their reflections in step 4].'
   • 'One thing I will do to deepen my discipleship is [complete this sentence from their reflections in step 5].'
   • 'One thing I will do to support the life of our church is [complete this sentence from their reflections in step 8].'

   They should take the card away with them as a reminder of their commitment, for prayer and action.

11  To finish, ask everyone, 'If we were faithful in these small steps, what difference would it make to our community and beyond?' Note some of the responses, and incorporate these into the closing prayers.

## What next?

Arrange a feedback session for participants to share their stories of change. This both encourages people and helps build confidence, and also provides accountability.

The leadership of the church may also want to consider the various suggestions. Make sure that the group all know how the information shared during the exercise will be used from the outset, and that you have permission to share anything discussed.

## Variations

If time is short, steps 3 and 4 can be omitted.

# Now What?

Having employed some of the activities explained in the previous pages, you may find that they have served a valuable purpose in and of themselves. No obvious follow-up is needed. At other times a foundation has been laid and some of the other activities available here may help to build on what has already occurred. In such cases the 'What next?' section at the end of activities you have already used may highlight some helpful possibilities for next steps.

## Turning dreams into reality

The outcomes of some facilitated activities with a congregation or group comprise ideas, possibilities and hopes – the beginnings of a vision that demands faithful action in response. One definition of 'vision' is 'a preferred future'. When people have vision, they imagine and desire a situation which is different from the status quo. Perhaps, for example, previously unnoticed opportunities or overlooked needs may have been identified. Sometimes these seeds of vision are expressed with clarity and backed by a broad consensus; at other times it may be manifest as some vague ideas or glimpses of what might be. Either way, whether clear concept or imprecise inklings, this final section provides some pointers to take the next steps in ways which optimise the chances of intentions becoming reality.

## Clarification and affirmation

When insights or ideas emerge from the prayers, reflections and conversations of any group of people they must be treated with the value and respect that they deserve. Those with responsibility to lead the group or congregation need to affirm the outcomes of the process, clarify them and do what is needed to turn vision into reality. In practice this will mean planning: deciding the how, when, by whom, with what resources and so on are necessary if ideas are not to remain just ideas.

If the hope and momentum created by the shared activities are to be maintained and bear fruit, it is important that those involved in the process (and those in the group or congregation who were not involved) hear, as soon as possible, that the outcomes have been considered by those with leadership responsibilities, have been affirmed and that steps are being taken towards implementation. The rest of this section is intended to help ensure that the move from dream to reality, from vision to implementation, is as smooth and as effective as possible.

## Navigating change and transition

Too many excellent decisions are never implemented; too many sound ideas never progress from the drawing board to actuality; too many sound plans fail, or create unnecessary problems because of a lack of wisdom in how they are put into practice. When there is vision there must inevitably be change. This may be minor or major in scale. It may involve initiating something new, stopping something existing, or making adjustments to something current. Understanding some principles about human nature and how people and groups behave in relation to change is helpful in creating consensus and commitment – and avoiding unnecessary misunderstanding and conflict.

Change, even when it seems minor or inconsequential to some, will have an emotional impact. When changes occur to what we do as a group or congregation, how we do things, or when physical changes are made to buildings, different people respond in different ways. For some, a particular change will be like embarking on a fresh and exciting journey, something they anticipate with eager excitement. For others, the very same change may cause anxiety and a sense of loss; they may strongly disagree with the proposed change. Any change will bring with it an experience of 'transition' as individuals, groups or a congregation come to terms with the change and what it means for them.

In many ways 'change' is the easy bit. 'Transition', the psychological process people go through to come to terms with change, is the difficult part. For most people change is perceived as a loss before it is experienced as a gain. For this reason, we can't initiate a process of change without creating a grief reaction in people – however irrational this may sometimes seem.

People need to understand, therefore, that how they implement change will have a significant impact on people's experience of transition. How we manage change and transition pastorally will shape the culture of the group or congregation into the future. The following insights and tips will help to introduce change while avoiding unnecessary pain and struggle.

# Communication

The single most important piece of advice about introducing any kind of change, whether small or huge, is this:

**Communicate, communicate, communicate … and when you think that you have communicated enough, communicate some more**

Communicate a picture of the future (vision); communicate the purpose of change and the reasons for change; communicate clearly regarding the part that people have to play; communicate in every possible way and many times. Don't just include a note in a bulletin or a post on a Facebook page and think that everyone will read it and understand. Use every means possible to communicate clearly several times.

If there are changes that are planned that are in any way complex, controversial or expected to be difficult for some people, it is a good idea to have people specially assigned to the task of communication, including having time to spend with people individually when that is necessary.

# The change formula

Experts in managing change in commercial and charitable organisations have observed that, for change to take root and be fruitful, certain conditions need to be present. The same is true in the context of churches and Christian organisations. These have been expressed in what is known as 'the change formula'[6]:

$$C = D + V + FS + E > £$$

To translate into everyday language, it means:

Change = Discontent + Vision + First steps + Energy – which must be perceived to be greater than the cost involved.

Before embarking on a particular change it is worth reflecting on these factors. Is there sufficient discontent with the current situation to make change worthwhile? Or/and is there really a commitment to the vision for this? Is there clarity around the first steps that will be necessary? Is there the energy to carry it forward? And will the cost be justified? The 'cost' may include time, money, emotional costs or closing the door on other alternatives.

# Understanding reactions to change

In any group of people it is usual to find that, in regard to any particular change, there will be a spectrum of reactions. At one end of the spectrum, there will be a few people who are passionate advocates for the change. At the other end of the spectrum there may be some who will remain intractably opposed to any change.

In the middle of the spectrum we usually find the majority. They will embrace the change if it seems to be the right way forward and is well communicated. They will reject the change if they fail to see its benefit, don't understand it or sense that it may be harming individuals. A key to introducing change then is to communicate effectively with the majority rather than rush ahead with the enthusiastic few.

It is worth noting that it is at either end of the spectrum that the volume level tends to be highest. It is important not to be intimidated by those who are loudest. They are operating out of strong emotions and intuitions. The people in the middle tend to be relatively quiet and respond to careful and reasonable explanation: what? why? how? when? who? how long? and how much? Effective implementation of change requires patience in winning the quieter, reasonable majority. Once a course is plotted we need to be entirely consistent with that new heading. However, the pace at which we advance needs to be sensitively managed to encourage those not yet committed to get on board and to avoid unnecessary stress.

# Quick wins

It is important then that everyone can see some tangible outcomes as soon as possible. The 'Where Do We Start?' activity on page 138 provides a helpful tool for analysing the outcomes of a facilitated process in terms of their expected impact and the inputs required.

| | |
|---|---|
| High impact<br>Low cost<br><br>*Quick win* | High impact<br>High cost<br><br>*Strategic* |
| Low impact<br>Low cost<br><br>*Debatable* | Low impact<br>High cost<br><br>*Avoid* |

Obviously changes that are perceived as having a low impact will need to be debated carefully. Especially if they require a lot of input, whether in time, money or any other resource, then it is probably best to avoid them altogether. Many long-term, high-impact changes will require considerable resources. These are the big, strategic changes that take long-term commitment and may require new resources. Often though there are some changes, which, although they are perceived as high impact, actually require relatively little in terms of time and other resources. These are the 'quick wins' – changes that should be implemented promptly. As people see these things becoming reality it will encourage them that change is possible, that the facilitated activities or process is bearing fruit and that there is a commitment to seeing things through.

## Experiments

Most major changes will have their advocates and their opponents. However, many opponents are unsupportive because they are genuinely unconvinced about the suggested benefits. Many, although they will resist commitment to a plan they feel is unwise, will not be averse to trying something for a limited period or on a small scale in order to see whether the hoped for benefits materialise or not. There is, therefore, much to commend the idea of time-limited experiments or trials.

## Sending out the spies

It is unlikely that any of the ideas that have emerged have never been tried or implemented by others. There can be considerable benefit in doing some detective work to find other groups or churches that have tried something similar and in then going and seeing for yourself. Just as Moses sent out the spies to investigate the Promised Land, you may be able to send a team to visit a situation where similar things are being done. Include a mix of people in the team: men and women of different generations and not just the enthusiastic advocates of what has been suggested. Then, after the visit, get the team to feed back their findings.

As mentioned in 'Facilitation Made Easy' on page ix, part of the vision behind the book in your hands is a network of facilitators who support and learn from one another, inspire and encourage each other. Please join the Building the Body Facebook Group at: www.facebook.com/Building-the-Body-735800873453062 and, as things develop in your situation, do share your experiences.

# Notes

1 The theory of Transactional Analysis can be traced to the work of American psychotherapist Eric Berne.

2 Ready-made cards are available from coaching resource suppliers (e.g. Barefoot Coaching or Thinkwave), where they are usually called 'Picture Coaching Cards'. Some public service providers use such cards for similar purposes, e.g. NHS Scotland have an excellent set of 'Envision Cards' available for free download. Otherwise you can create your own cards by collecting images from magazines or online sources. The website www.writingexercises.co.uk has a random image generator from which pictures can be freely downloaded. www.upsplash.com has thousands of good quality images that are freely available, as long as you remember to credit the photographers and, if appropriate, include a link to their web space.

3 Terrence Deal and Allan Kennedy, *Corporate Cultures: The Rites and Rituals of Corporate Life* (Reading, MA: Addison-Wesley, 1982).

4 See www.knowledge.scot.nhs.uk/media/CLT/ResourceUploads/4087782/0a49abf1-3524-4894-9302-86a976d8ee44.pdf.

5 J. Campbell, *The Hero with a Thousand Faces* (London: Fontana Press, 1993).

6 The 'change equation' was first articulated by Richard Beckhard and Reuben Harris, based on an idea by David Gleicher. See R. Beckhard and R. T. Harris, *Organizational Transitions: Managing Complex Change* (Reading, MA: Addison-Wesley, 1977).